Orchids
of the North Woods

By Kim & Cindy Risen

T0151304

Kollath+Stensaas
PUBLISHING

Kollath+Stensaas Publishing
394 Lake Avenue South, Suite 406
Duluth, MN 55802
Office: 218.727.1731
Orders: 800.678.7006
info@kollathstensaas.com
www.kollathstensaas.com

ORCHIDS *of the* NORTH WOODS

Printed in South Korea by Doosan
10 9 8 7 6 5 4 3 2 1   First Edition

Editorial Director: Mark Sparky Stensaas
Graphic Designer: Rick Kollath

Illustrations by Rick Kollath, Kollath Graphic Design
www.kollathdesign.com

ISBN-13: 978-0-9792006-7-0

Table of Contents

Dedicated to our children
Shaila, Shirin & Cody

In memory of our sisters
Rene & Laura

Precious blossoms all

Acknowledgements

I want to thank my parents, Burton and Margie Anderson, who taught me how to enjoy the outdoors and encouraged a curiosity about the life around me.

Audrey Engels and Rolf Dahle, my mentors, who, along with Karen Myre, spent many an hour explaining the intricacies of orchids and *Botrychiums* sometimes in the pouring rain, the hot sun or knee deep in bogs. I learned a great deal and formed wonderful friendships.

The late Janet Boe, Minnesota Department of Resources Regional Plant Ecologist, who let me tag along while conducting plant surveys near my home. She shared friendship and kindness along with her wealth of knowledge.

—Cindy Risen

Cindy, my True Companion on our most important journey—life. Floating bogs, cedar swamps and sphagnum carpeted cathedrals with their magical orchids; sunrises over the Amazon Basin; hummingbirds, tanagers and orchids beyond belief amidst South America's Andes; beaches, birds, butterflies, Mayan ruins and orchids across the Yucatan Peninsula; boat rides through mangroves and exploring back roads to small Mexican villages; Lions, Hippos, Elephants and African sunsets. All were special because you were there to share them with me. You have me always looking forward to our next great adventure.

My parents, Duane and Judy Risen, who opened the door. My earliest memory is of the outdoors. Strolling through fields and woods with my father, fishing pole in hand, stopping to admire every little thing that caught a two-year-old's eye. Bravery is letting your children explore, discover and learn all that a back 40 has to offer—whether it's a bubbling spring, dark swimming hole or rabid raccoon. If that's not bravery, dozens and dozens of camping, fishing, hunting, berry picking or picnic trips with seven kids most certainly is!

Dave Hanson, who lit the spark—photography, birds, flowers. Proving that introducing youngsters to the wonders of the natural world has a lifelong impact.

John Wild & Chuckie Whelan Wild, whose infectious enthusiasm for orchids proved contagious.

—Kim Risen

Welby Smith, who provided an expert voice in answering so many questions. Erika Rowe gave us field-experienced feedback on our Minnesota range maps.

Sparky Stensaas, our friend and publisher, who gave us an opportunity to share our photographs and enjoyment of orchids...not to mention his positive attitude, gentle guidance and enduring patience. And to Rick Kollath, for his wonderful illustrations.

Warren Nelson, for sharing his knowledge of birds and plants with others.

The Peter Schmidt family, for sharing the rare orchid in their backyard.

For help locating orchids: Rolf Dahle, Audrey Engels, Jim Tranna, Warren Nelson, staff of the Minnesota DNR for sharing orchid sites and information about state parks and scientific and natural areas, Minnesota Nature Conservancy's Matt Mecklenburg, Sonia Winter and staff for their information, guidance and stewardship.

Bob DuBois, whose introduction to biological classification was an inspiration.

Thanks to the photographers who shared their exceptional photos. This book was made more complete because of their efforts.

—Kim and Cindy Risen

May 11, 2010

Preface

THERE IT IS! Our reaction to finding an orchid is always the same—excitement and wonder. We're not alone in that. Orchids have long held a position of high esteem, their reputation as exotic beauties justifiably earned.

Orchids are stereotypically viewed as gaudy flowers inhabiting steamy tropical jungles in some distant land. While true—orchids are the largest family of flowering plants with staggering diversity in tropical climates worldwide—they're well represented across the North Woods region as well. Orchids in the frozen northland? Oh, yes! Including some of the world's most beautiful examples. Discovering how many orchids thrive in the North Woods is eye-opening to many.

True field guides—references meant to be carried and used while trudging through bogs, forests and swamps—can hold only so much information. We wanted *Orchids of the North Woods* to be a field guide. We introduce you to each native orchid you could encounter here, showing you when and where you could expect to find them, sharing identification tips, educating you a bit about their biology and providing a few interesting tidbits to better appreciate each species uniqueness.

We're avid birders. Finding and identifying birds, keeping lists and searching out the next species to add to your collection of sightings can be a large (and fun!) part of the birding game. For many, including us, it's the same with orchids. Pleasure felt upon discovering a new orchid is motivation driving you to find the next. Each find an exhilarating addition to a growing list of treasures. Spotting an orchid is one of life's simple pleasures, no matter if it's the first orchid you've found, a commonly encountered friend or a highly sought rarity.

Photographing these amazing plants can be a significant element of enjoying orchids. It sure is for us. Working out the challenges associated with capturing a pleasing photo can be a difficult task. Compiling a bit of what we've learned over the years, we've included a "How to Photograph Orchids" primer to help you in your flower photography.

This is the guide we wished we had on our first outings so many years ago. And it is MEANT to be used. Please, tuck it in your back pocket, toss it in your daypack or slide it into your camera bag. Just be sure to take it with you on your next North Woods hike, bike, paddle or walk.

Introduced to the wonders of nature at a young age, we're fortunate to have grown up in the North Woods with its amazing birds, butterflies, wildlife and colorful orchids all around us. May you, too, find the natural attractions of the North Woods as compelling as we do. We hope our guide delivers a bit of understanding and brings you much joy of discovery!

Enjoying Orchids

There is in each North Woods season, save the depths of winter, fun orchid watching opportunities. That's why we've included leaves of our evergreen species and seed pods—find them when little else is growing, mark their location and return to see them in bloom.

An incredibly diverse region, North Woods landscapes contain many orchids. Visiting these fascinating bogs, swamps and woods should be your goal. Advance study prepares you for which orchids you're likely to find at your chosen destination and time. Learn their field marks, fix that 'search image' in your mind and test your powers of observation.

Looking for orchids is easy, finding them is a bit more difficult! Luckily, this is a learned skill that improves with use. Best tip we can offer is to go slowly, watch where you walk and, when possible, get low. When you find an orchid, crouch down and take a closer look at the area. You'll be amazed at your new discoveries!

The list of gear or equipment for orchid watching is short: Orchids thrive in habitats where it's easy to lose your way. Hiking through thick cedar swamps or featureless bogs with your eyes upon the ground, make a compass or GPS an indispensable tool and knowing how to use them a mandatory skill. A sufficiently detailed map of the area you're visiting should receive equal billing. Know where you are, where you are going and how you will return BEFORE you enter that dark cedar swamp!

We've enjoyed heated debates about the 'proper' footwear to use during an orchid outing. It comes down to one of two schools of thought, boots or old shoes? We disagree, so it's your choice!

Binoculars or, even better, a hand lens are extremely useful. You'll soon learn they open an entirely new perspective on our native orchids. What at first glance may be taken for an unattractive and entirely uninspiring flower, under the magnified view of a hand lens becomes a natural marvel of function and beauty.

The North Woods is filled with insects, its mosquitoes the stuff of legend! Ticks, particularly Deer Ticks, offer dangers of their own in the form of Lyme's Disease. Add hoards of Deer Flies and other biting insects to the mix and the need for protective measures becomes painfully obvious. We enjoy good results by wearing long-sleeve shirts and applying insect repellant to all exposed skin. Tuck your pants into your rubber boots or socks and apply repellant to your lower legs to reduce the number of ticks hitching a ride. A head net is particularly helpful when taking photos or spending extra time in one spot.

Finally, enjoy your search, have fun and share your knowledge and enthusiasm by introducing a child to our wondrous orchids of the North Woods.

What is an Orchid?

What is an orchid? That's a difficult question to answer. Most simply, any member of the orchid family is, by definition, an orchid. However, as orchids belong to the largest living group of flowering plants on the planet a complete answer becomes a bit more complex.

Let's go back to your high school biology class. You may recall discussing Carl Linnaeus and his development of a revolutionary classification system that changed how we look at the natural world. Remember, big groups, like kingdom, phylum and class, were parked at the top of the chart supported by progressively smaller categories, as genus and species, toward the bottom. A remarkably simple system whose defined ranks brought order to the chaos of all living things. That simplicity, with many adaptations over the centuries, allows us to wrap our minds around the staggering complexity and diversity of life on our planet. Linnaeus's system is still the standard more than 350 years after its introduction.

Carl Linnaeus, the father of modern taxonomy.

Mr. Woodington, my biology teacher, gave us the mnemonic device

What isn't an Orchid...Beware the Imposters!

There are a few wildflowers you may encounter that upon first glance could be mistaken for an orchid. Beware the imposters! Fringed Polygala (*Polygala paucifolia*) is an early blooming pink-blossomed beauty that you will find in the company of pines. Cousins Indian Pipe (*Monotropa uniflora*) and Pinesap (*Monotropa hypopitys*) are both saprophytes that lack green chlorophyll as in some orchids (*Corallorhiza*/Coralroot species). A cursory examination will quickly separate these imposters from true orchids.

Pinesap (*Monotropa hypopitys*)

Fringed Polygala (*Polygala paucifolia*)

Indian Pipe (*Monotropa uniflora*)

"**D**o **K**ids **P**refer **C**heese **O**ver **F**ried **G**reen **S**pinach" insuring that we'd never forget the order of Linnaean taxonomical ranks: **D**omain, **K**ingdom, **P**hylum, **C**lass, **O**rder, **F**amily, **G**enus, **S**pecies. It's worked for me, even decades removed from class.

Where do orchids fit within this system?

Containing complex structures within its cellular walls, orchids are assigned to the **Domain** (Superkingdom) Eukaryota.

Orchids reside in the **Kingdom** Plantae and—along with trees, herbs, grasses and mosses, to name a few—are considered true plants.

Traits such as flowers, seeds enclosed within a fruit and a vascular system with vessels put orchids in the **Phylum** (Division in botany) Anthophyta (or Magnoliophyta). Drawn from Greek *anthe* meaning flower and *phyto* meaning plant, thus 'flowering plants.' Also known as angiosperms which derives from Greek *angeion* meaning 'vessel' or 'enclosure' and *sperma* meaning 'seed' referring to the group's trait of seeds encased within fruit.

Orchids are housed within the **Class** Monocotyledonae. Members are called Monocotyledons or monocots for short. Their name is taken from *mono* meaning 'one' or 'singular' and *cotyledon* or 'seed leaf,' which is an organ within the seed of a plant. Home to nearly one fourth of all flowering plants on earth, monocots include several large groups of plants—agaves, grasses, lilies, orchids and palms.

The **Order** Asparagales is a cosmopolitan one, composed of mostly herbaceous perennials of about 30 families and nearly 30,000 species.

Characteristics of monocots:
- Embryo with single cotyledon
- Major leaf veins parallel
- Flower parts usually in multiples of three
- Pollen with single furrow or pore
- Stem vascular bundles (vein system's primary trunks moving water and nutrients through the plant) are scattered

Characteristics of Orchids:
- Stamens and pistils (male and female parts) fused together into a single structure unique to orchids known as a column
- Modified stigma known as rostellum serves to transfer pollinia to pollinators, frequently through amazing methods
- Three petals and three petal-like sepals usually with one highly modified petal called the labellum or lip
- Flower stems twist as they develop via process called resupination
- Pollen usually in masses known as pollinia
- Seeds are tiny, numerous and lack endosperm (food supply)

In addition to orchids, it includes asparagus, daffodils, irises, day lilies and foods like garlic, leeks and onions.

Family Orchidaceae, the orchids, is the largest family of flowering plants on earth. Name derives from Greek *orchis* meaning 'testicle' in reference to the shape of tubers found on some orchids.

Genus (plural genera) is from Latin *genus* meaning 'descent, family or type' and is a taxonomic rank that groups closely related species together. Currently there are nearly 900 described genera of orchids worldwide, with the North Woods home to less than 20 of them.

Species (plural species) is the most basic of the eight major taxonomic ranks. While there are over 25,000 described species of orchids worldwide, many more remain undiscovered or undescribed, especially in highly diverse tropical regions.

Lesser taxonomic ranks like **subspecies**, **variety** and **forma** are used to recognize variation within a particular species. Subspecies and variety indicate more substantial deviations with forma designating minor differences. Subspecies and varieties generally have a defined geographical range and produce offspring that resemble the parent; forma are more likely individual variations occurring randomly within any population.

An orchid by any other name...

If you try to include the entire scientific name starting with kingdom, phylum etc., full names quickly become impossible. Instead, in everyday usage only the 'binomial' (two names) portion of an orchid's name is utilized. Binominal refers to the simple pairing of genus and species. The genus is listed first (its first letter capitalized) followed by the species name (or specific epithet), uncapitalized. Binomials create readily understood scientific names used by botanists, amateurs, professionals, orchid enthusiasts and naturalists alike.

Common names are often as confusing as they are helpful. Frequently referred to as 'English' names, they aren't standardized and they're used inconsistently. Changing between regions, generations, people and authors, a hodgepodge of common names has arisen. We found more than ten common names for some species and a few examples of the same common name applied to different species!

Folks using scientific names aren't snobs trying to impress others with their intellect. It's just that by using the binomial system, people discussing a particular orchid can be reasonably certain they're discussing the same species. So, while common names may seem easier to use at first, effort should be made to recognize different genera and use scientific names. Besides communicating effectively you'll be able to impress others with your grasp of a dead language!

Orchid Biology 101

All our orchids are considered terrestrial in that they take root in soil. There are minor exceptions, *Malaxis paludosa* usually has its roots suspended within sphagnum, never quite reaching true soil and *Goodyera repens* has been found growing amid moss atop decaying trunks of ancient fallen trees.

In orchids, one flower petal (the lip or labellum) is highly modified in shape, color and structure; usually to aid in insect pollination.

You know that orchids are monocots and, like others in that large group, typically have flower parts in groups of three or six. Orchid flowers have three sepals and three petals, with one petal, the labellum or lip, that's highly modified in color, shape or structure. The lip acts as a landing pad or guide, directing an insect to its stored nectar and pollen. A result of their evolution to attract particular insect pollinators, these often fantastically altered lips provide orchids their exotic beauty. Sepals vary in color and form, some species match the brilliant petals while others are a simple green.

Unique to orchids is the fusion of the male/stamen and female/pistil reproductive parts into a single structure called the column. Located at the center of the blossom opposite the lip, the column is responsible for completing pollination as an insect brushes against it enroute to the nectary. The column can direct pollinators of the correct size into the exact position required to receive any pollen it may be carrying or to deposit pollen upon it before it departs. The various shapes, enticements and orientations of the lip, column and pollinium illustrate the high degree of specialization used by orchids during reproduction. This results in isolating mechanisms that are behavioral and physical in nature, both are barriers that act as identifying characteristics to determining species.

Unlike most plants that produce a dust-like pollen the consistency of powder, orchids generate large masses of pollen called pollinia. Attached to either side of the column, pollinia become attached to an insect when that insect touches the sticky gland. As it leaves, the entire mass of pollen becomes attached to the insect and is transported to the next flower it visits. Transferring large quantities of pollen in a single visit has its advantages—the more pollen that's delivered the better the chances of effective fertilization.

Orchids are an amazingly large group of plants with many agents to act as pollinators. In addition to the usual bees, butterflies, flies, gnats, moths and wasps, pollination is assisted by hummingbirds, wind, rain

Parts of an Orchid

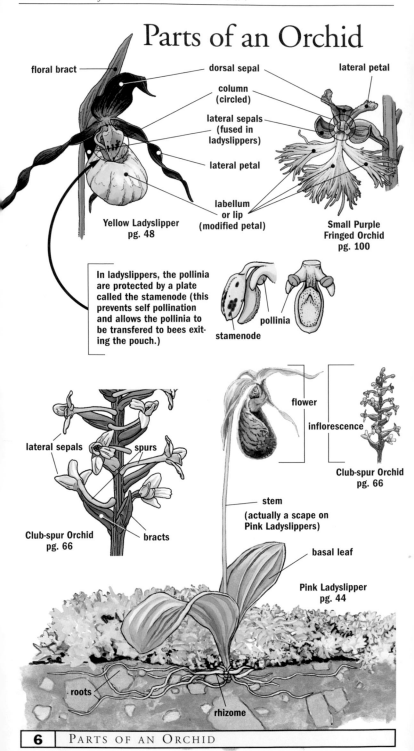

floral bract

dorsal sepal

lateral petal

column
(circled)

lateral sepals
(fused in
ladyslippers)

lateral petal

labellum
or lip
(modified petal)

**Yellow Ladyslipper
pg. 48**

**Small Purple
Fringed Orchid
pg. 100**

In ladyslippers, the pollinia
are protected by a plate
called the stamenode (this
prevents self pollination
and allows the pollinia to
be transfered to bees exit-
ing the pouch.)

pollinia

stamenode

flower

inflorescence

**Club-spur Orchid
pg. 66**

lateral sepals

spurs

stem
(actually a scape on
Pink Ladyslippers)

basal leaf

**Club-spur Orchid
pg. 66**

bracts

**Pink Ladyslipper
pg. 44**

roots

rhizome

and, when all else fails, some are even self-pollinating. Regardless of the type of pollinator, most orchids have developed relationships with one particular type or species to the point that when its pollinator disappears, so does the orchid.

While most plants have an ovary surrounded by floral structures at the center of the flower, orchids have an ovary that's situated beneath the flower resembling a swollen stem. As the ovary ripens into fruit it becomes filled with seeds. Orchids produce the smallest seeds of any flowering plant with a typical seed pod holding hundreds of thousands or even millions of seeds. These minute seeds are covered by a thin protective cellular wall and lack a stored food source called endosperm. While their lightweight construction allows them to be spread widely by wind and water, the lack of protection and food reserves results in a dreadfully vulnerable seed subject to a high loss rate.

With no self-contained food source, seeds require the assistance of a most unique partner—fungi living within the soil! The fungus enters the seed, attaching itself to the embryo and providing the nutrients necessary for the seed to germinate and grow. All orchids form lifelong partnerships with these fungi through a relationship known as mycorrhiza. These nearly invisible fungi are vital to the growth and continued development of all our native orchids. They 'infect' the orchid through threadlike hyphae that penetrate the orchid's roots. Within the orchid, the fungus is consumed as food—first to induce the germination of seeds, then to maintain seedlings as they develop and finally in sustaining the health of adult plants. Upon reaching maturity, most orchid plants are able to obtain food through both photosynthesis and its root fungus. However, *Corallorhiza* members generally lack chlorophyll, relying entirely upon their fungal partners for their nutrient supplies. It is this fragile mycorrhizal relationship that makes orchids difficult (if not impossible!) to transplant from the wild. When an orchid is removed from an area holding its required fungal sidekick, the plant will decline and die, starving from the severing of the fungal-orchid partnership.

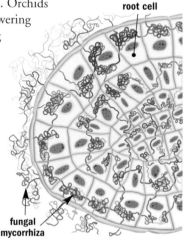

orchid root cell

fungal mycorrhiza

Illustration at a microscopic scale of fungal hyphae inside an orchid root tip. The mycorrhiza of the fungi provides nutrients to the developing orchid.

Orchid Genera of the North Woods

The bird people have their act together—at least when it comes to standardization of common and scientific names. The world of botany could learn a thing or two from them. There is no single botanical organization that has the ability to standardize names. This leads to controversy and inconsistency in the naming of orchids and other plants. Systematics is the science of classifying organisms according to their phylogeny—their place on the evolutionary 'family tree' of life. Continually in flux as new discoveries cause changes in our understanding of plant relationships, systematics is best described as a snapshot of our knowledge at a particular moment in time. Accordingly, the list of orchid genera is continually changing as taxonomists discover, learn and debate plant relationships. Currently there are about 900 genera of orchids recognized worldwide. Below are the genera included in this book.

Amerorchis — Round-leaved Orchis

A single-species (monotypic) genus endemic to the more northerly habitats of North America.

Generic name derived from a combination of *Amer* for America and *orchis* for a widespread genus of Old World orchids, thus meaning American Orchis.

Orchis is a large and confusing group of European orchids that's proved problematic to taxonomists for a long while. While Orchis comes from Greek meaning 'testicle,' only Old World members of the genus have testicle-like bulbs. *Amerorchis* lacks these tuberoids and was separated from the poorly defined Old World genus in 1968.

Specific *rotundifolia* means 'round leaf,' for the round shape of its basal leaves.

Aplectrum — Puttyroot

Single-species genus endemic to eastern North America, although an extremely similar species occurs in Asia.

Generic *Aplectrum* comes from Greek, *a* (without) and *plectron* (spur), describing the flowers' lack of spurs. Specific *hyemale* means 'of the winter' after the solitary leaf that persists through winter.

Origin of common name Adam-and-Eve is from the presence of two connected corms. The previous year's old, withering corm doesn't disappear, it remains connected to the new one by a short rhizome. Thus, the younger corm springs forth from the older, as Eve from Adam's rib. The orchid's current season's grown rises from the newer corm, Eve.

Arethusa — Dragon's Mouth

Single-species genus endemic to eastern North America, although the closely related *Eleorchis japonica* of Japan was formerly treated as con-generic *Arethusa japonica*.

Named for beautiful fountain nymph Arethusa, 'the waterer.' In Greek mythology, she was the daughter of Nereus (making her a Nereid). A fitting name for this orchid given its beauty and preference for watery habitats.

Specific *bulbosa* derived from Latin meaning 'bulbed,' referring to its small pseudobulb.

Dragon's Mouth

Calopogon — Grass-Pinks

Endemic genus to North America with five species recognized. Only one, with two geographically sepa-rated varieties, occurs in the North Woods.

Generic *Calopogon* drawn from Greek *kalos* and *pogon* which translates as 'beautiful beard' in description of the multi-colored lip hairs.

Thriving in wet bogs, grassy meadows and marsh edges, *Calopogon* is an indication of good water quality. At one time was assigned to the genus *Limodorum* which could be loosely translated as 'meadow gift', a particularly poetic designation for this wet meadow dwelling beauty.

Pollination of *Calopogon* is a fascinating process demonstrating the marvelous complexity of orchids. Unlike most orchids, the lip is situat-ed at the top of the flower, a feature described as non-resupinate, mak-ing it look upside down—because it is!

Pink coloration and brushy yellow hairs adorning the lip act as irre-sistible lures to gullible bees. Searching for pollen or nectar, bees are drawn to the upsidedown lip with these hairs acting as pseudopollen decoys. Upon landing, its weight on the hinged lip causes it to quickly drop down, with the bee helplessly along for the ride it becomes trapped against the column. Flaring wings on each side of the column prevent the ensnared bee from escaping to either side, forcing an exit off the end. As the stigma smears the bee with a glue-like material, pressure from the struggling bee pushes the pollen masses out of their protective pocket. As the bee finally escapes the trap, sliding off the column touches the exposed pollen to the bees sticky belly. Instantly hardening, the glue cements the pollen to his abdomen and, pulled from their pocket as the bee leaves, are now in the perfect location to land on the stigma of the next *Calopogon* he tumbles into—*Viola!*, cross-fertilization is achieved.

One of only a few flowers which mechanically move the insect to the

Tuberous Grass-Pink (*Calopogon tuberosus*) has evolved into a master deceiver. A bee searching for pollen is attracted to pollenless yellow fringed hairs on the lip.

As the bee lands, the hinged lip collapses under the weight of the bee. This is one of only a few flowers that actually physically move their pollinator.

stigma, *Calopogon* adds insult to injury as the bees receive no sweet reward for their misadventures. Victims quickly learn to boycott the plants, requiring a new supply of recently emerged, inexperienced bees.

Calypso — Fairy Slipper

Single-species genus composed of four wide-ranging varieties, one of which occurs in the North Woods. Each variety fills its own geographic zone across the circumboreal distribution of the genus.

Named for a sea nymph from Homer's Odyssey. Calypso, the beautiful daughter of Atlas, kept Ulysses concealed on her island Ogygia for seven years. It also means 'hidden' or 'concealed.'

Calypso

The singular beauty and rarity of *Calypso*, its hidden nature and the seclusion of its preferred cedar haunts, make the name appropriately descriptive.

Specific *bulbosa* derived from Latin meaning 'bulbed,' referring to its small pseudobulb.

Coeloglossum — Frog Orchid

Single-species genus composed of several varieties, only one occurring in the North Woods. Circumboreal in distribution, it utilizes a wide variety of boreal, forested and mountainous habitats.

Generic derived from Greek *koilos glossum* which translates as 'hollow tongue,' describing the small, hollow spur at the base of tongue shaped lip. Specific *viride* and varietal *virescens* both derived from Latin meaning 'green,' referring to its bright green flowers.

Origin of common name 'Frog Orchid,' is unknown. We've found two descriptions, neither is very convincing. Perhaps as, with a great

The bee falls back onto the column where it is coated with a sticky substance by the stigma. Further struggling causes pollen packets to adhere to the bee.

Upon escaping, the bee may pass on pollen from a previous Grass-Pink, or if this is his first visit to such a flower, then he may pollinate the next one visited.

deal of imagination, the flower's shape resembles that of a leaping frog. Another possibility, the flower's silhouette looks like a frog with the multi-lobed lip suggesting the frog's hind legs and the sepals cupped over the column its body.

Recent studies have suggested that *Coeloglossum* may be placed within the genus *Dactylorhiza*. However, conflicting opinions exist and the view is not universally accepted. Most authorities continue to recognize them as two closely related but distinct genera.

Corallorhiza — Coralroots

A primarily American genus with 13 species spread across temperate regions of North and Central America. One enjoys circumboreal distribution with four species occurring in the North Woods.

Generic derived from Greek *korallion* meaning 'coral' and *rhiza* meaning 'root,' which describes the rhizome's appearance to that of a coral formation.

All *Corallorhiza* are leafless mycotrophic (fungus feeding) plants. Instead of obtaining food on their own via sunlight, they obtain food (organic carbon) and nutrients from a host green plant with an assist from an intermediary—a mycorrhizal fungus attached to its roots.

While all orchids require these mycorrhizal fungi to complete critical stages of their growth, *Corallorhizas* continue to require them their entire lives. Most coralroots do not produce chlorophyll, becoming dependent upon these fungal associations for nourishment. The yellow-green species, *C. trifida* and *C. odontorhiza*, are notable

The underground rhizome's coral-like appearance gives rise to the common name and genus name.

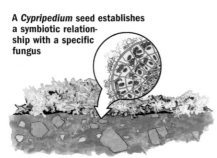

A *Cypripedium* seed establishes a symbiotic relation- ship with a specific fungus

A protocorm slowly develops underground, perhaps 3 to 7 years, living on starches provided by the fungi. Once it has grown a root system, a bud is produced.

It takes a dozen years or more for

exceptions. Possessing trace amounts of chlorophyll, they're able to photosynthesize at least minimally, resulting in reduced dependance upon their fungal partners.

This reduction or lack of chlorophyll is why they lack leaves and produce stems and flower parts in often brilliant shades of purple, pink, red and yellow.

Not relying upon sunlight for their nutritional needs, members exhibit dramatic fluctuations from year to year in their aboveground numbers. Most of the time, a majority of them remain underground. Living as a perennial rhizome nourished by these fungi, they rise to bloom only under favorable conditions.

Cypripedium — Ladyslippers

Widespread genus containing some of our most captivating and well-known orchids. Their muddled taxonomy continues to evolve with about 50 species currently recognized. Growing across temperate North America, Europe and Asia, these are some of our most hardy orchids, established on Siberian tundra, Dakota prairies and virtually every habitat in the North Woods. North America boasts twelve members, five call the North Woods home.

It's generally accepted that the generic is an incorrectly Latinized version from the Greek, *Kypris* 'Venus' and *podion* 'slipper' or 'Venus's slipper' or 'little foot' thus 'lady's slipper.'

Ladyslippers have three petals one of which, the lip, is modified into the trademark slipper. These vividly colored slippers make them our most easily recognized group of orchids. Pinpointing a universally accepted name is difficult, a sampling of common names include Camel's Foot, Lady's Slippers, Moccasin Flowers, Slipper Orchids, Squirrel Foot, Steeple Cap, Venus' Shoes and Whip-poor-will Shoes.

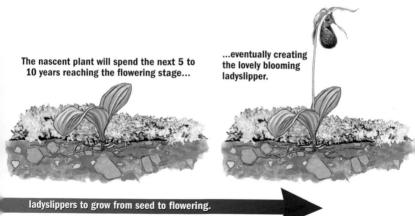

The nascent plant will spend the next 5 to 10 years reaching the flowering stage...

...eventually creating the lovely blooming ladyslipper.

ladyslippers to grow from seed to flowering.

Uses deception to attract pollinators—the flower looks and smells like an attractive food source but offers no nectar in reward.

Pollinated by bumblebees who, enticed by the blossom's color and odor to enter the pouch, become entrapped. In-rolled edges at the slipper's opening make it impossible for the bee to exit the way it entered. Contrasting colored lines and hairs inside the pouch direct the hapless bee to a pair of openings at the rear of the slipper. As it leaves, the bee passes under the stigma depositing any pollen it may be carrying, thus completing cross-pollination. In order to prevent self-pollination, the bee doesn't come in contact with the blossom's pollen supply until after it passes the stigma and forces its way out of its trap. Passing under exposed pollinia, a new mass of pollen is deposited on the bee as it finally escapes.

Bees quickly learn from their misadventures and avoid *Cypripedium* flowers. Thus, like several North Woods orchids dependent upon inexperienced, naive bees, they generally experience low pollination rates. Luckily, ladyslippers consistently reproduce vegetatively, sending up shoots from horizontally creeping rhizomes. Our benefit? Crowded clusters of blossoms to admire!

Most are slow growing, taking a decade or more to grow from seed to blossoming plant. Luckily they're long lived if not disturbed. Large plants, with dozens of flowering stems may total a hundred years or more.

Foliage of several species causes an itching rash similar to poison ivy in some people. A trait that has aided in catching orchid poachers!

In the wild, several species have become quite rare as habitat loss, climate change and unscrupulous collecting have all taken their toll. In recent years, progress has been made in the commercial propagation of *Cypripedium* so we can all hope that collecting of native orchids from the wild may become a thing of the past.

Dactylorhiza (see *Coeloglossum*)

Epipactis — Helleborines

Widespread genus of Europe, Asia and Africa with only a single species native to North America. A second species, introduced from Europe, has become established across much of eastern North America.

Generic evidently derived from Greek *epipaktis* or *epipegnuo*, ancient Greek names for Hellebore, a traditional name for the genus.

Has spread rapidly since its introduction to North America in the 1870s. First discovered in New York in 1879, it's now listed as occurring in 39 states and provinces.

Galearis — Showy Orchis

Small genus containing two disjunct species. One found in eastern Asia the other, from eastern North America, occurs in the North Woods. Formerly considered part of the overly inclusive genus *Orchis*.

Generic *Galearis* drawn from Latin *galea* meaning 'helmet' referring to the helmet-like hood formed by the sepals and petals.

Goodyera repens

Goodyera — Rattlesnake-Plantains

Widespread genus holding approximately 25 species around the globe. Four species occur in North America, all can be found in the North Woods. While one is circumboreal in distribution, *G. repens*, it's represented in our region by a distinct variety.

Genus was named for famed 17th-century English botanist John Goodyer (1592-1664).

Goodyera members are easily recognized by their basal rosette of handsomely marked leaves. As these leaves resemble those of Common Plantain (*Plantago*) the group is often referred to as 'plantain' orchids. Members are also referred to as 'rattlesnake orchids.' We've found several descriptions for the origin of this common name: network of markings on each leaf mirror the pattern found upon the back of a rattlesnake; OR densely packed racemes resemble the tail of a rattlesnake; OR densely packed seed capsules, when dried, rattle like a rattlesnake. Pick your favorite!

Goodyera tesselata

Goodyera pubescens

Goodyera oblongifolia

Most can be identified by their leaves:

G. repens—smallest leaves, less than 1.5 inches (38 mm) long, heart or egg-shaped, dark green with pronounced white veins in an all-over web-like pattern.

G. tesselata—medium length leaves, up to 2 inches (5 cm) long, narrow, pointed oval in shape and leaves are light green and indistinctly patterned.

G. pubescens—second largest leaves, up to 4 inches (10 cm) long, broad pointed oval in shape, bright green with sharply contrasting web of thin, pale markings along veins and a pronounced wide, white center vein.

G. oblongifolia—largest leaves, up to 4.5 inches (11 cm) long, gently pointed oval in shape with distinctly wavy/wrinkled edges, dull blue-green with obvious wide, white center vein usually without reticulation. At times there may be some webbing on the leaves, but it's never to the extent of other *Goodyera*.

Goodyera hybrids and backcrosses are surprisingly common, with most intermediates generally unidentifiable. This penchant for hybridizing is responsible for the creation of an entirely new species. *G. tesselata* has its origins as a hybrid between *G. oblongifolia* x *G. pubescens*. Interestingly, the hybrid has outdistanced one of its parents as *G. tesselata* is common in Minnesota, but *G. oblongifolia* has yet to be confirmed for the state!

Gymnadeniopsis — Frog Orchids
(split from *Platanthera*)

A genus composed of three species, one occurring in the North Woods. Formerly included within *Habenaria* then, after the separation of *Habenaria* and *Platanthera*, within *Platanthera*. Now described as a distinct genus differing from *Platanthera* on the basis of roots with tubers and small, projecting tubercles on the column. What a difference a few bumps can make!

Generic drawn from Greek meaning 'similar to *Gymnadenia*.' A closely related genus of European orchids, *Gymnadenia* derives from Greek *gymn* meaning 'gland' and *aden* meaning 'free' describing the free or uncovered viscidia.

Club-spur Orchid: as the flowers develop they twist about 180 degrees—some a little more and some a little less.

Liparis — **Twayblades**

Widespread genus comprising some 250 species worldwide. Reaching their greatest diversity in tropical climes, only three species are native to the continental U.S. and Canada, two of these occur in the North Woods region.

Generic is from Greek *liparos*. Origin for lipid and liposuction, it translates as 'fat,' 'greasy,' 'oily' or 'shining.' As root of *Liparis*, it's in reference to the leaves of most members of the genus which are smooth and shiny or wet in appearance.

Both North Woods species produce distinctive seed capsules that greatly outlast their blossoms, allowing easy identification long after the blooms have disappeared. Can be distinguished from closely related *Malaxis* by their elongated columns.

Listera — **Twayblades**

Compact genus of about 25 species enduring cooler, temperate and boreal environments of Northern and Southern Hemispheres. Eight species live in the U.S. and Canada, five species call the North Woods home.

Genus named for prominent English naturalist and physician Martin Lister (1638-1711). Generally small and nondescript, all members exhibit two opposing leaves, giving the group their common name of twayblades. Lips of flowers are prominently forked or two-lobed and, as most have sepals and petals that curve backward, their distinctive lips are pushed center stage. Size requires the use of a hand-lens to see details of these petite flower parts.

Listera auriculata

North Woods twayblades are easily separated by lip shape:

Listera auriculata - lip more or less rectangular with parallel sides, slightly 'pinched' in center. Moderately notched, about one fourth its length, with diagnostic basal auricles clasping the column.

Listera convallarioides

Listera convallarioides - broad lip, only slightly notched, producing two shallowly rounded lobes, wide at tip narrowing dramatically, but evenly, to a slender attachment at the base.

Listera cordata - lip very short, deeply forked (about half its length) dividing the lip into two narrow, pointed lobes.

Listera cordata

Twayblades utilize a shared pollination mechanism that even Charles Darwin found fascinating. Nectaries on the lip produce small amounts of nectar that attract small, flying insects. Moving about the lip, they trip microscopic hairs that act as triggers causing the rostellum to squirt a bit of glue onto the insect. Pollinia are instantly released over the glue with the quick drying cement anchoring them in place. When the insect departs, pollinia go along for the ride waiting to be deposited upon the next flower visited. In order to prevent self-pollination, the stigma will remain covered for about a day after losing its pollinia. It gradually becomes exposed allowing pollination to take place.

Malaxis — Adder's-Mouths

Widespread genus, most diverse in Asia and East Indies, with 250 to 300 species worldwide. Fifteen species occur in North America north of Mexico, three call the North Woods home.

Malaxis taken from Greek *malakos* meaning 'softening' or 'weak' referring to their soft, tender and often fragile nature.

Common name 'Adder's-mouth' comes from appearance of the flowers. In many species, the sepals and petals pull back, pushing the lip and pollen-bearing column forward. While affording pollinators better access, the arrangement gives plants a look resembling the mouth and tongue of a snake.

Characteristically, members of *Malaxis* are small and nondescript with the genus holding some of the smallest flowers of any orchid on the planet, often no larger than a few millimeters across. Because of their small size, flower detail is best viewed with a hand lens. Often going undetected, even botanists consider several species rare or little known. All species possess a pseudobulb.

Piperia (folded into *Platanthera*)

A taxonomically confusing genus endemic to North America formerly recognized on its own, but now included within *Platanthera*. First recognized in 1901 when similar *Habenaria* and *Platanthera* species were brought together into the newly created genus named for botanist Charles V. Piper. Shared characteristics include scant basal leaves, slender bracts on the stem and a raceme of quite small flowers with spurs. Of the ten former *Piperia* found across western North America, only one occurs in the North Woods.

Relatively recent efforts to fold *Piperia* back into *Platanthera* on the basis of DNA analysis are now generally accepted. However, the former name of our North Woods dwelling Slender-spire Orchid, *Piperia unalascensis*, still enjoys wide use.

Platanthera — **The Bog/Fringed Orchids**

Widespread genus across temperate habitats of Northern Hemisphere. Holding about 45 species, this is the largest group of orchids in United States and Canada. It enjoys a similar position in the North Woods, with 11 species regularly occurring in the region.

Generic drawn from Greek *platys* meaning 'broad or wide' and *anthera* meaning 'anther,' describing the separated base of the pollinia typically exhibited by members of the genus.

First described in 1818, the genus has known, and continues to undergo, much revision—but little consensus! Removed from overly inclusive *Habenaria* in 1972 with characters as the absence of stigmatic processes and ovoid root-tuberoids considered the most compelling. After the split, *Platanthera* became limited to temperate climes with *Habenaria* now restricted to subtropical and tropical regions. The genus continues to be the subject of much scrutiny and within the last few years a number of opinions have been published that advocate substantial changes to *Platanthera* and it closest relatives. Only time, and additional research, will prove which is most convincing.

Rose Pogonia

Most utilize full sun and deeply shaded haunts equally. Sun loving plants tend to be shorter, have more flowers packed along their stems and produce leaves that grow more vertically. Shade dwellers are just the opposite, tending to grow taller, with fewer flowers along a loose raceme and more spreading leaves. Individual flowers remain unchanged.

These are some of our largest and most ornate orchids, often producing tall, flower-filled spikes. The fringed orchids stand out as most impressive members of this splendid group.

Pogonia — **Pogonia Orchids**

Relatively small genus composed of three or more species (depending upon which taxonomic choices you make). Most diverse in East Asia, only a single species occurs in the New World, but it's particularly well distributed across Eastern North America. In the correct habitat, under ideal conditions, it's a common resident of the North Woods often seen with pitcher plants, sundews and grass-pinks.

Generic *Pogonia* is derived from Greek *pogon*, meaning 'beard,' and describes the bearded surface of the lip.

Aromatic, raspberry scent and bright coloration are inducements for pollinators, bumblebees, to visit. Ultraviolet markings direct them to the correct position on the lip so that during its search for a deceptively small nectar reward pollination occurs.

Spiranthes — Ladies'-Tresses

Widespread genus of temperate habitats across northern hemisphere. While about 25 species occur in North America north of Mexico, only five can be found in the North Woods.

Generic *Spiranthes* drawn from Greek *speira* meaning 'coiled' and *anthos* meaning 'flowers' that describes the typical spiral arrangement of blossoms along the stem. This repeated spiral pattern resembles tightly braided hair in a French braid thus the common name Ladies'-tresses.

With distinctive twisted spikes of white or creamy-white flowers Spiranthes are some of the easiest orchids to identify to genus. Frustratingly, minute differences between some species means they are also some of the most difficult to identify to species!

DON'T COLLECT!

Whether novice or expert, professional or amateur, searching for (and spotting!) these unique flowers is great fun—a pure and simple pleasure to be enjoyed by all. We're fortunate that the North Woods holds many beautiful native orchids. They should be considered natural treasures, regarded as a most precious resource.

All our native orchids live in close association with specific fungi that are required for each orchid to germinate, sprout, grow and thrive. Such fungi rarely live away from where you find native orchids growing—a primary reason why you found the orchid growing in the out-of-the-way location you did and NOT in your backyard!

For these reasons and more, native orchids should NEVER be collected! 'Collect' the orchids you encounter by taking photographs or keeping a checklist of those you've seen. PLEASE, leave our native orchids to thrive in the wild places you find them so that others may experience the same thrill of discovery as you.

Orchid Photography

Photography of a subject that's quite literally rooted in place may seem to be a straightforward task, it's often more difficult than you would think. Many orchids have tiny flowers and grow in dark wet areas. Certainly not ideal circumstances for photography.

Photography is all about capturing light. Some orchids prefer dark forests and bogs where light is in woefully short supply, others grow only in full sunlight. Both situations offer challenges. Bright overcast conditions are ideal. Why? Well, there's plenty of light and the high clouds diffuse the sunlight so that there's no harsh shadows, yet the light retains the texture, character and subtlety of your subject.

Luckily, you can take light away when there's too much of it. Direct sunlight is horribly contrasty. It creates black shadows that lose their detail and ghastly burned out highlights in the lit areas. This problem is most severe when photographing white flowers.

What to do? You need to reduce contrast, and there are two easy methods: use a portable diffuser or white umbrella in place of clouds to diffuse the sunlight by holding it several feet above the orchid; or simply put a little extra light into the dark areas by reflecting light from the sun or your flash into the harsh shadows.

Conversely, you add light when there's too little of it by using a reflector or a flash to put light on your subject. This fill-in light reduces harsh shadows while increasing the three dimensional look of your subject.

There are many commercially available reflectors. Gold reflectors add warm light to the subject with silver adding cool. Or you can make your own by simply taping aluminum foil to a piece of cardboard.

In dark cedar bogs, where little light reaches the forest floor, using a

4 Do's

- Be picky! Always choose the best flower specimen available. If you don't see what you want, keep looking. You definitely want the one orchid that's so impressive it begs to be photographed!

- Get low. Eye-level photographs offer more intimate views of your subject and you can even shoot parts of an orchid.

- Watch your background. Distractions—bright sunlit areas, tree trunks, branches—can destroy an otherwise excellent photo. Use larger apertures to create soft out-of-focus backgrounds. You can create a dark background by using flash that lights the subject leaving everything behind the orchid black.

- Experiment. Try a variety of camera angles and positions. Create something beyond a standard portrait for more dramatic photos.

4 Pieces of equipment...other than your camera

- Tripod or bean bag for support (using it is a must!)
- White diffusing umbrella (or two), extremely versatile tools—you can use it as a diffuser, you can bounce fill-flash off of it and it works great as a wind block.
- Light reflector(s) of your choice—try one, you'll like it!
- Bug spray, towel and extra batteries—you'll see.

flash becomes your only option. A flash mounted away from the camera works better and, if you have the equipment, using one flash on the subject and one on the background yields ideal results.

White, pale or lightly colored flowers present special problems. Often the easiest solution is also the best, simply reduce the power of your flash or move it or your reflector farther away. Also, aiming them to one side often adds a softer sidelight that works well.

While an SLR camera and matched macro lens may be the best way to capture close-up photographs of orchids, many of today's digital point-and-shoot cameras also take remarkably good flower photos. Most have a close-up or macro setting, appropriately, the commonly used icon for this feature is a flower!

Eliminate camera movement by using a tripod, bean bag or some kind of support. Eliminate subject movement by using your umbrella as a wind block. Check your focus point insuring that autofocus locks on your desired subject. Watch your background, watch your lighting.

A small tripod (or large tripod that goes low) and a diffuser (white umbrella) can go a long way in making better orchid photos.

Don't step on, or place your tripod on, an orchid or its roots. Don't remove surrounding vegetation, if its in the way, tie it back or hold it to the side temporarily. A little housekeeping by removing dead/movable objects like leaves or pine needles is okay.

Digital photography provides two big benefits and you should take advantage of them. First, check your pictures right away. See what's working for you and what isn't. Experiment, change your camera settings until you get the photo you want. Secondly, memory is far less expensive than film, so take lots of photos and have FUN!

How to use this Field Guide

Orchids of the North Woods is designed to make field identification easier for you, the reader. Through the use of color photos of the entire plant, close ups of individual flowers, rare or unusual color forms, seed capsules and leaves, we have created a unique guide that highlights the orchid traits you are most likely to see in the field and need for proper identification. Detailed range maps help you narrow your search. This handy, compact and easy-to-use guide is small enough to tuck into any daypack.

Coverage
More than 50 species of native orchids occur in the North Woods. We cover them all...including six species that are at the fringes.

Names
Latin and common names are given for all species. Even botanists and their professional organizations don't agree on common names (and even genera placement) of our native orchids. The authors have used the most widely accepted names from other published sources. *Other Common Names* lists alternative names; colloquial and regional.

Phenograms
The red bar phenograms show the range of flowering dates for that species. Peak flowering dates are likely in the middle of the red bar, but remember that microhabitats and latitude can vary bloom phenology for individual species by days to weeks.

Habitat
Our region enjoys a wide variety of habitats due to the geological features created, transformed and imprinted upon the landscape by glaciers scouring the continent during the last glacial age. It's this variety of bogs, fens, meadows, seeps, swamps and forests that allow orchids to thrive, each in their own, often highly specialized, niche. Below the phenogram we list the favored habitats of that orchid.

Range
Broad, brief, descriptions describe North American distribution as it relates to the extent of eastern, western, northern and southern ranges. Species with worldwide distribution are noted. Circumboreal species likely occur in Scandinavia, Siberia/Russia, Canada and possibly China and Japan.

Where to Look

The authors have tramped many miles of backcountry bush and bog in search of orchids. From Michigan to Minnesota, Kim and Cindy have sought orchids in their home habitats. Here they share some of their laboriously acquired hotspots—all on public land, of course—and tips to help you find every orchid species.

Nature Notes

Fascinating facets of natural history are included here. Also the orchids special status in Minnesota, Wisconsin and Michigan are noted ('Species of Special Concern,' 'Threatened' or 'Endangered').

Maps

Detailed maps of Minnesota, Wisconsin and Michigan highlight in pink the current known range of each species. Our knowledge of species range changes daily. Report sightings of out of range orchids to a local university.

Main photo is often a close up of a single flower (or basal leaves of the rattlesnake-plantains)

Phenogram highlights when that species is blooming

Rare or unusual color forms may be shown here

Photo of entire plant

Side photos often show a seed capsule

Nature Notes **are natural history tidbits about that species**

The orchid's favored habitats are shown here

Genus name in Latin and English is listed on the bottom of each page

Maps highlight in pink the current known range

Small Round-leaved Orchis
Amerorchis rotundifolia

dark color form

APRIL	MAY			AUG	SEPT	OCT

Calcareous cedar/tamarack/spruce swamps amid deep sphagnum moss.

Nature Notes:

Endemic to arctic and boreal habitats of North America.

While it can be abundant in scattered northern locales, it's most easily found in Minnesota.

Amerorchis is 'Endangered' in Michigan and 'Threatened' in Wisconsin.

Can be abundant in spots.

Showy, coveted and highly photogenic resident of forested peatlands and sphagnum carpeted coniferous forests.

Other Names: One-leaf Orchid, Round-leaved Orchis/Orchid.

Description: 3 to 14 inches (7–36 cm).

Variable terminal raceme with up to 18 white to pale pink blossoms. Spurs are shorter than the lip and slightly curved. Seed capsules are ellipsoid, about 0.6 inches (1.5 cm) long.

Flowers: Small nickel-sized blossoms. Three-lobed lip elegantly freckled with magenta. No two blossoms are identical. At times red-purple spots merge forming two heavy bands along the lip (inset photo) or, at the other extreme, are lacking completely producing snowy white flowers.

seed capsules

Leaves: Solitary, shiny green leaf sheaths the stem at its base. The conspicuous ovate leaf is present during flowering.

Similar Species: None.

Reproduction: Much of the biology of *Amerorchis* remains a mystery. Studies have shown *Amerorchis* flowers to be nectarless and scent-free thus the plant probably relies upon self pollination and vegetative reproduction.

Range: Alaska east to Newfoundland and Greenland, south to Wyoming, northern portions of Great Lakes states from Minnesota east to northern Maine.

Where to Look: The extensive peatlands of north central Minnesota offer your best chances of finding *Amerorchis*. Surprisingly large numbers await those brave enough to explore away from roadside ditches. Don't forget your compass or GPS!

Puttyroot
Aplectrum hyemale

APRIL	MAY		JULY	AUG	SEPT	OCT

Mixed deciduous woodlands with rich, moist soils.

Nature Notes:

Common name is for heavy, sticky fluids obtained from crushed tubers used by early Americans to repair pottery and as glue.

Frequent ingredient in folk medicine; dried corms are used to cast love charms, worn as amulets to insure fidelity in a mate and used to tell your fortune.

Listed as a 'Species of Special Concern' in Wisconsin.

While it can occur in colonies numbering in the hundreds, only a few plants produce blossoms come flowering time.

Odd, shade loving orchid of southern deciduous forests, rarely found in the North Woods.

Other Names: Adam-and-Eve, Eve-and-Adam.

Description: 7 to 20 inches (18–50 cm).

A loose terminal raceme sporting 5 to 16 flowers rises from two connected corms.

Flowers: Small blossoms about ½ inch (1.3 cm) long framed by similar yellow-green sepals and petals that fade to darker maroon or purple at their tips. The whitish, three-lobed lip is wrinkled along its lower edge and variably marked with darker maroon/purple.

Leaves: Puttyroot's most distinctive feature is the lone blue-green basal leaf. It is large, pleated and oval, generally 3 to 7 inches (8–18 cm) long by 1 to 3 inches (2–8 cm) wide. Resembling a greenish corn husk, the sterile

flower buds

seed capsules

leaf appears in late summer, stays green through winter and withers as flowering begins.

Similar Species: Resembles coralroots, the leafless stem is more yellowish than green.

Reproduction: While pollination by small bees of the genus *Dialictus* has been documented, studies show that assisted pollination in the wild is infrequent. Self-fertilization, asexual seed formation without fertilization and vegetative reproduction are all utilized.

The single rounded blue-green basal leaf is Puttyroot's most distinctive feature.

Range: Minnesota east to southern Ontario and Vermont, south to Oklahoma, Arkansas and Georgia.

Where to Look: Most easily found during late fall or winter when their distinctive, erect leaves provide the only green on the forest floor. Return in June to see the blooming orchid.

Dragon's Mouth
Arethusa bulbosa

APRIL	MAY			AUG	SEPT	OCT

Open sphagnum bogs, fens, sedge meadows and floating bogs.

Nature Notes:

'Species of Special Concern' in Wisconsin.

Dragon's Mouth is considered rare over most of its range, being listed as rare in 17 of the 21 states and 6 of the 9 provinces where it occurs.

Because *Arethusa* is an early successional species, it disappears when shrub cover becomes too thick.

Early Americans used the corms of *Arethusa* to treat toothaches.

Widely adored, exotic looking jewel, considered one of our most beautiful native orchids.

Other Names: Swamp-pink, Wild Pink, Bog Pink, Bog Rose.

Description: 3 to 16 inches (7–40 cm).

Flower: Large, 1 to 2 inch (2.5–5 cm), blazing pink-purple flower. Rectangular, wavy and downward arching lip is marked with white, darker magenta and yellow and crowned with distinctive fleshy 'hairs.' Sepals and petals stand erect like the ears of an alert animal or, perhaps, like the horns of a dragon? Variable white and purple forms.

Leaf: Generally absent at flowering time; single grass-like leaf 5 to 10 inches (12–25 cm) long develops after the flower fades.

Similar Species: Beyond utilizing the same

rare white form

habitat, blooming at the same time and being pink, Rose Pogonia and Tuberous Grass-Pink really aren't that similar and flowering plants shouldn't be confusing. Calypso Orchid blooms much earlier and prefers shaded cedar swamps.

Reproduction: While pollinated by bumblebees of the genus *Bombus*, it appears that pollination in the wild is infrequent and, because they're susceptible to frost, seeds may not be produced every year. *Arethusa* reproduces asexually, spreading slowly from its bulbous tubers.

Range: Southern Manitoba east to Newfoundland, Minnesota south to northern Indiana and northern South Carolina.

Where to Look: Northern Minnesota's peatlands and sphagnum bogs are considered a stronghold for the species and numbers in the tens of thousands are possible. While common on floating mats around northern lakes, where they may grow to the waters edge, extra care needs to be taken when searching to insure you don't break through.

Minn.

Wisc.

Mich.

Tuberous Grass-Pink
Calopogon tuberosus var. tuberosus

APRIL	MAY	JUNE	JULY	AUG	SEPT	OCT

Open coniferous swamps, floating mats & sedge meadows with ample water.

Nature Notes:

Tuberosus describes its thick, tuberous roots.

One of our few native orchids that grows easily from seed without a symbiotic mycorrhizal relationship. Accordingly, they're popular with gardeners and can be purchased commercially. Just make sure the plants are cultivated stock and not poached from wild populations.

Its presence is an indicator of high quality surface and ground water.

At one time was assigned to the genus *Limodorum* which could be loosely translated as 'meadow gift.'

Biological marvel that loves water, thriving in saturated sphagnum and grasses, lending blazing color to the landscape.

Other Names: Grass-Pink, Common Grass-Pink, Grass Pink Orchid.

Description: 4 to 22 inches (10–56 cm).

Terminal raceme (highly variable in height and number of flowers) grows from a bulbous corm loosely entangled within a wet substrate. Capsules, erect, rounded ellipsoids 0.5 to 1.25 inches (1–3 cm) long.

Flowers: A showy cluster of 2 to 15 sweet-smelling blossoms that bloom in slow succession up the stem. Blazing pink to pale purple (rarely white), 1 to 2 inches (2.5–5 cm) in size. Lip uppermost; anvil-shaped brandishing conspicuous yellow-tipped bristles and poised

flower bud

seed capsules

above a narrow, curved column cupped within the brilliantly colored sepals and petals.

Leaves: Usually one erect, grass-like leaf strongly ribbed with parallel veining. Long, 2 to 20 inches (5–50 cm), and narrow.

Similar Species: Shouldn't be confused with any other northern orchid.

Reproduction: Pollinated by small bees via an extraordinary process (see text page 9 and illustrations pages 10-11).

Range: Manitoba east to Nova Scotia and Newfoundland, south to Texas and Florida.

Where to Look: Widespread throughout the North Woods. We've found them most easily on 'floating bogs' that border many of our boreal lakes and open spruce swamps. Plan on getting wet feet while searching and bring an extra pair of socks!

Minn.

Wisc.

Mich.

Calypso Orchid (Fairy Slipper)
Calypso bulbosa var. americana

APRIL	MAY	JUNE	JULY	AUG	SEPT	OCT

Cool, moist and heavily shaded old growth cedar or fir/spruce forests.

Nature Notes:

Calypso is threatened in both Wisconsin and Michigan.

Corms were used as a food source by native peoples and, in British Columbia, the Thompson River Indians used it to treat mild epilepsy.

Elusive and ephemeral beauty, a near mythical resident of pristine coniferous woodlands.

Other Names: Venus's Slipper, Angel Slipper, Deer's-head Orchid, Hider-of-the-North, Redwood Orchid.

Description: 2 to 9 inches (5–22 cm).

Flower: Small, scoop-shaped lip less than an inch (<2.5 cm) long, whitish with dark maroon markings. Front portion is spoon shaped with two obvious horns below and a striking yellow beard above.

Leaf: The single basal leaf, a pleated oval 1 to 2 inches (2–6 cm) long, appears in late summer. It persists through winter, withering shortly after flowering begins in spring.

basal leaf

Similar Species: Similarities are faint, but Dragon's Mouth is also pinkish with erect petals/sepals and a yellow beard.

Reproduction: Plants are intolerant of soil temperatures above 59 degrees F (15 C) or canopy covers less than 60 percent and live no more than five years. Reproduction is sexual and asexual with pollination needing assistance among ten species of bumblebees identified as pollinators. A dormancy period of several years is common.

Range: Circumboreal. Occurs Alaska east to Newfoundland, south in western mountains to California, in the Rockies to Arizona and across Great Lakes from Minnesota to Maine.

Where to Look: In late May, check thick cedar stands in Northern Minnesota or make an adventure of your search with a visit to Isle Royale National Park. When wandering off trail, be sure to have your compass or GPS.

Minn.

Wisc.

Mich.

Long-bracted Orchid
Coeloglossum viride var. virescens

APRIL	MAY	JUNE	JULY	AUG	SEPT	OCT

Rich, acidic soils of shaded, moist, hardwood and coniferous woodlands.

Nature Notes:

Flowers tilt downward to the point that it's often hard to tell if the plant is, in fact, blooming. No worries, an eye-level inspection quickly answers the question and, while you're down there, you can take a few photos!

Natives found assorted uses for the roots—in ceremonies, as a love charm, as an aphrodisiac and as a gynecological aid.

Widespread, but easily overlooked, shade loving orchid often found along roadsides and trails.

Other Names: Long-bract Frog Orchid, American Frog Orchid, Long-bract Green Orchid, Bracted Bog Orchid, Satyr Orchid.

Description: 4 to 22 inches (10–56 cm)

Leafy stem rises from a palmate tuber. Capsules elliptical, erect, less than 1/2 inch (<1.3 cm).

Flowers: Terminal raceme tightly packed with up to 75 petite, yellowish green flowers. Flowers subtended by prominent, pointed leaf-like bracts.

Rectangular lip may be tinged purple, notched with three tooth-like projections—two longer points on each side framing a shorter one in the middle. Petals and sepals curve up and in forming a cupped hood over the lip. Small, sack-shaped spur, hard to see.

Leaves: 2 to 6, broadly oval. Leaves 2 to 6 inches (5–14 cm) long, alternately clasp the stem; upper leaves smaller, narrower and more pointed.

Similar Species: Several *Platanthera* orchids are look alikes; prominently cleft, strap-shaped lip and lack of a obvious tubercle distinguish it.

Reproduction: American variety not as well known as European. Self-pollinated by pollen falling from crumbling pollinia landing on stigma. May be pollinated by small bees, beetles or wasps.

Range: Circumboreal. Eurasia. Alaska east to Newfoundland, south to Washington and in mountains to Arizona and New Mexico, Nebraska east to Maine, south in Appalachians to North Carolina.

Where to Look: Tolerates disturbance well, rarely found in mature woods. We've had good luck in state parks and reserves with established trail systems. Search thickets and shrubby borders of trails. When you find one, take a close look around, we wager you'll find more close by!

Minn.

Wisc.

Mich.

Genus *Coeloglossum* FROG ORCHID | **35**

Spotted Coralroot
Corallorhiza maculata var. maculata

APRIL	MAY	JUNE	JULY	AUG	SEPT	OCT

Rich, dry to moist, acidic soils in wide variety of upland forests.

Nature Notes:

Two varieties occur here: var. *maculata* (Spotted Coralroot) and var. *occidentalis* (Western Spotted Coralroot.) Western tends to bloom 2 to 4 weeks earlier, has more flowers packed on the raceme, has longer, often forked, floral bracts and is typically redder stemmed. Most easily told by lip shape: rectangular with parallel sides is Spotted, broadly rounded at the tip is Western.

Coralroots live most of their lives underground, flowering only when conditions are ideal—blooming in abundance one year, nonexistent the next.

Curious, colorful, common and highly variable orchid of woodlands across the region.

Other Names: Large Coral-root, Spotted Coral-Root, Summer Coralroot.

Description: 6 to 26 inches (15–66 cm).

Smooth, colorful scape rises from brittle, coral-like branching rhizome. Capsules drooping ellipsoids less than an inch (< 2.5 cm) long.

Flowers: 5 to 50 small, less than 1/3 inch (<8 mm) long, flowers on a loose, reddish-purple to yellowish raceme. Slightly cupped, maroon and white flowers face forward. Sepals and petals reddish-purple fading to yellowish basally. Three-lobed lip with wavy front edge is whitish, variably spotted red to purplish. Much variation in stem and flower coloring and lip spotting.

seed
capsules

Leaves: No real leaves, reduced to a few over-lapping, inflated bracts sheathing the stem.

Similar Species: While coralroots look similar, differences in blooming time, flower shape and coloring tell them apart.

Reproduction: While *Empis* dance flies and andrenid bees are reported pollinators, it's typically self-pollinating with most flowers bearing fruit.

Color forms are varied;
Here is a yellow form
with an unspotted lip.

Range: SE Alaska east to Newfoundland, south to California, west Texas and Iowa, east to Maine, south in Appalachians to north Georgia; also Mexico and Central America.

Where to Look: Search mixed, mature hardwood forests, usually in deep to semi-shade. The brightly colored stems stand out surprisingly well. We've found them easily in state parks of NE Minnesota and NW Wisconsin, including our favorite—Savanna Portage State Park!

Minn.

Wisc.

Mich.

Autumn Coralroot
Corallorhiza odontorhiza var. odontorhiza

APRIL	MAY	JUNE	JULY	AUG	SEPT	OCT

Rich, calcareous soils of moist, upland deciduous woods.

Nature Notes:

Specific, *odontorhiza*, combines two Greek words meaning 'tooth root' describing a tooth like growth extending from its rhizome.

Listed as a 'Species of Special Concern' in Wisconsin.

Got roots? Not coralroots. They only have rhizomes (an underground stem) and lack true roots.

Even healthy populations experience dramatic fluctuations in above ground numbers. Most plants stay underground as perennial rhizomes, emerging only under ideal conditions.

Bizarre mycotrophic orchid occurring above ground infrequently—a rootless, leafless, flowerless wonder.

Other Names: Late Coralroot, Fall Coralroot, Small-flowered Coralroot.

Description: 4 to 11 inches (10–28 cm).

Lacking chlorophyll, the purple to brownish, rarely yellow, terminal raceme with 15 to 16 loosely spaced flowers grow from a rootless coralloid rhizome. Bulging ovaries rapidly develop into hanging capsules about ⅓ inch (8 mm) long.

Flowers: The small flowers (about ⅛ inch (3 mm) long) rarely open. Swollen ovaries and ripening capsules are its most obvious feature. When visible, the lip is rounded with wrinkled edges and white with dark purplish spotting.

Leaves: Lacks leaves, though bladeless sheaths laying flat along the stem may resemble leaves.

seed
capsules

Similar Species: Variety *C. o. pringlei,* is identical save production of typical, open flowers, generally occurs southeast of the North Woods. Oft confused Early Coralroot resides in northern bogs, has a greenish stem and is done blooming by July. Much larger Spotted Coralroot displays brightly colored, flared open flowers.

Reproduction: Largely self pollinating as flowers do not open. Small insects pollinate plants that produce open flowers.

Range: Eastern North America from Minnesota east to Maine, south to Florida and Louisiana. A southern orchid; rare in the North Woods.

Where to Look: Rare and easily overlooked, its coloration and short stalks make them difficult to spot amid autumn's fallen leaves—if they're even visible (see Nature Notes). Often discovered by accident in the same areas as other mycotrophs like Spotted Coralroot, Indian Pipe and Pinesap. Reason enough for a fall walk through an upland forest. Enjoy the color, the season and the search.

Striped Coralroot
Corallorhiza striata var. striata

APRIL	MA		JULY	AUG	SEPT	OCT

Rich, moist soils; most often in shady coniferous or deciduous woods.

Nature Notes:

Specific *striata* is Latin meaning 'striped,' and describes the spectacularly striped sepals and petals.

Largest of North Woods coralroots, it tolerates cold but not heat restricting it to more northerly or mountainous regions.

Our showiest coralroot, exquisitely striped flowers resemble brightly colored candy rising from shadowy forest floors.

Other Names: Hooded Coralroot, Macrae's Coralroot, Striped Coral-root

Description: 4 to 20 inches (10–60 cm).

Stout, succulent scape rises from a fragile, coral-like rhizome, in clusters of a few up to twenty plants or more. Lacks chlorophyll, colored purplish to dark red or brown. Capsules drooping ellipsoids one half to one inch (13–25 mm) long, floral remnants often remain.

Flowers: 5 to 35 dime-sized, spurless flowers decorate the terminal raceme. Sepals and petals slightly concave and spreading, with striking dark red stripes. Dorsal sepal and petals hooded over lip. Lip scoop-shaped with broad reddish-purple streaks merging into solid color near tip.

Leaves: Coralroots have no leaves, but three to four paler, overlapping bracts sheathing the lower stem range from maroon to dull yellow.

Similar Species: In bloom, the red-striped flowers are unmistakable. When in bud, or when only fruit capsules remain, it may not be safely differentiated from Spotted Coralroot.

Reproduction: Pollination by parasitic wasps has been reported and self-pollination occurs commonly, but reproduction is mostly vegetative via spreading rhizomes. After blooming, may live entirely underground for several years before rising once again.

Range: British Columbia east to Newfoundland, south to California and Texas, northern tier of states from North Dakota to New York.

Where to Look: Cool bogs and upland forests often accompanied by cedars. When you find one, a close look around is likely to reveal more. We've found them easily in mature woodlands of state and national forests across the North Woods.

Early Coralroot
Corallorhiza trifida

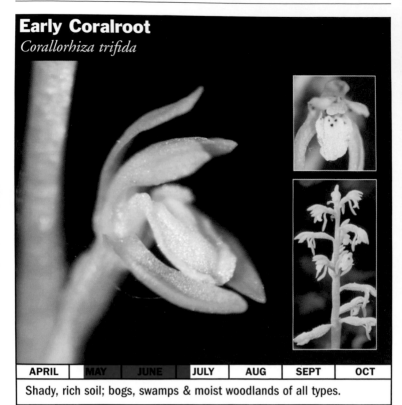

APRIL	MAY	JUNE	JULY	AUG	SEPT	OCT

Shady, rich soil; bogs, swamps & moist woodlands of all types.

Nature Notes:

Specific *trifida* drawn from Latin meaning 'three-cleft' or 'divided into three parts' in describing the three-lobed lip.

While all coralroots are mycotrophic and most produce no chlorophyll, the greenish coloration on its stem and all flower parts save the lip DO hold limited amounts of chlorophyll. Evidence that it may be capable of photosynthesis at certain stages of development thus reducing dependance upon its fungal partner.

Earliest blooming coralroot, an inconspicuous yet widespread orchid of forested peatlands and wet woods.

Other Names: Northern Coral-root, Yellow Coralroot, Pale Coral-root, Three-parted Coralroot, Spring Coralroot.

Description: 3 to 14 inches (8–35 cm).

Slender, yellowish-green scape rises from a branching, coral-like rhizome. Capsules pointed ellipsoids, large for flower size, up to ½ inch (15 mm) long droop at an angle away from stem often with withered flower remnants attached.

Flowers: 4 to 20 tiny, less than 3/8 inch (<1 cm), yellow to greenish flowers adorn a loose terminal raceme. Sepals and petals yellowish-green, hooded over the lip; petals shorter, thicker than sepals often with purplish spots. Lip white

flower bud

seed
capsules

(main photo) or white spotted with purple (inset photo), edges wavy with two small upturned teeth/lobes near midpoint.

Leaves: None, but several bladeless bracts sheath the stem's lower half.

Similar Species: Autumn Coralroot generally occurs south of North Woods and blooms much later—after Early Coralroot develops seed capsules. Spotted Coralroot blooms later, is distinctly larger with a noticeably spotted or purplish lip.

Reproduction: Chiefly self-pollinating. Pollinator observations rare; one report (from over a century ago!) was of a syrphid fly.

Range: Circumboreal. Eurasia; Alaska east to Newfoundland, south in mountains to California and New Mexico, Minnesota east to Maine, south to West Virginia.

Where to Look: Take a spring hike in your favorite North Woods park, keep your eyes moving and focused just above the ground. Often growing in tightly grouped clusters, their yellow stems stand out against the dark forest floor.

Minn.

Wisc.

Mich.

Pink Ladyslipper (Moccasin Flower)
Cypripedium acaule

APRIL	MAY — JUNE	JULY	AUG	SEPT	OCT

Poor, acidic soil, shade; dry, sandy pinewoods, wet coniferous bogs.

Nature Notes:

Specific derived from Latin *a* meaning 'without' or 'lacking,' and *caulis* for the plant's stem, thus meaning 'stemless' describing its lack of a visible true stem.

Provincial flower of Nova Scotia and Prince Edward Island.

A virtual pharmacopoeia, used by most eastern native American tribes in some way; roots used to treat menstrual disorders and venereal disease, infusion of roots used for colds, earache, stomachaches, kidney or urinary tract problems and as an ingredient to create 'love medicine.'

Colorful, primitive orchid of dark forests, bogs and swamps, one of our most familiar orchids.

Other Names: Stemless Lady's-slipper, Moccasin Flower, Pink Ladyslipper, Noah's Ark, Pink Moccasin Flower, Two-leaved Ladyslipper.

Description: 5 to 22 inches (13–56 cm).

True stem grows underground, a leafless scape rises between two leaves from course rhizomes. Capsules football-shaped, semi-erect up to 1.6 inches (4 cm) long. Green ripening to brown and prominently winged.

Flowers: Pubescent stalk topped by a nodding pink blossom. Sepals and petals greenish-yellow to reddish-brown, lateral petals twisting outward. Lip large, inflated pouch, up to 2.5 inches (6 cm) long. Top split with inrolled edges along its length. Gaudy pink to magenta

two-flowered
form

ripening
seed capsule

seed capsule

flourishing darker reddish veins; white and two-flowered forms are rare.

Leaves: Two (rarely 3) pubescent, strongly veined, green leaves grow direct-ly from rhizome sheathing scape at its base, up to 11 inches (28 cm) long.

Similar Species: Not to be confused with any other ladyslipper, its basal leaf pair and deeply creased, pink slipper are unique.

Reproduction: Pollination by bumblebees (see page 13) also propagat-ed by spreading rhizomes. Slow growing; seeds remain dormant until conditions are ideal—a wait that may last years—with first leaves not produced until several summers after germination. Seed to first bloom totals 8 to 10 years or more! (see pages 12-13)

Range: Northwest Territories east to Newfoundland, south through Minnesota to Alabama and Georgia.

Where to Look: Common across a wide variety of habitats. Impressive displays are found in most mature Tamarack/Black Spruce bogs. Don old shoes, apply bug dope liberally and enjoy your walk on the pillow-like sphagnum. Don't forget your camera!

Minn.

Wisc.

Mich.

Ram's-head Ladyslipper
Cypripedium arietinum

APRIL	MAY	JUNE	JULY	AUG	SEPT	OCT

Cool, weakly acidic soils in dense cedar/balsam/spruce swamps.

Nature Notes:

Specific *arietinum* comes from Latin meaning "like a ram." Get down to eye-level and use your imagination. Doesn't the pouch resemble the lowered head of a charging ram? You can even see the curly hairs between its ears!'

Listed as 'Threatened' in Minnesota and Wisconsin and 'Species of Special Concern' in Michigan.

Sometimes found in sand over limestone beach cobble or bedrock that's mulched with evergreen needles.

Dainty, rare and highly sought orchid of cool, dark swamps, bogs and woodlands.

Other Names: Ram's-head Orchid.

Description: 4 to 13 inches (10–33 cm).

A highly variable orchid with up to a dozen stems emerging from a common rootstock.

Flowers: Smallest flowers of any North Woods ladyslipper, about the size of your fingertip.
Leaves: Three to five mostly along the middle and upper portions of the stem covered with fine hairs and often folded.

Similar Species: None.

Reproduction: Long-lived perennial that doesn't flower until it grows to a height greater than four inches (11 cm). Flowers emit an aromatic scent in order to attract potential polli-

ripening
seed capsule

seed capsule

nators—small *Dialictus* and *Megachile* bees—who access the pollinia through the modified lip pouch. Within an hour or two of being fertilized, hormones induce the upper sepal to close over the opening of the pouch, like a trap door, preventing additional entry.

Range: Saskatchewan and Manitoba east to Nova Scotia, south to Minnesota east across the Great Lakes region and New England.

Where to Look: Ram's-head is famously difficult to see. Its general rarity, small size, camouflage coloration and irregular flower production are all contributing factors. Want to find your own? Try searching upland cedars in early June. Walk slow and watch your step!

In the rare form *albiflorum*, the slipper is whitish with pale green and translucent veining and pale yellow-green colored petals and sepals.

Minn.

Wisc.

Mich.

Small Yellow Ladyslipper
Cypripedium parviflorum var. makasin

APRIL	M~~A~~		JULY	AUG	SEPT	OCT

Wet habitats; conifer swamps with sphagnum, bogs, fens & meadows.

Nature Notes:

Listed as a 'Species of Special Concern' in Wisconsin.

Formerly treated as part of *Cypripedium calceolus*, which is now considered restricted to Eurasia, and known as *Cypripedium calceolus var. parviflorum.*

Charming, sweet smelling and small-flowered ladyslipper of diverse, moderately moist habitats.

Other Names: Lesser Yellow Lady's-Slipper, Northern Small Yellow Lady's-Slipper.

Description: 6 to 17 inches (15–43 cm).

Stems, often 10 or more, rise from a thick, spreading rhizome sprouting many fibrous roots. Capsule erect, prominently ridged ellipsoid up to 1.2 inches (3 cm) long, tops stem, flower remnants often remain.

Flowers: Single (rarely 2 or 3) small, vivid yellow flower nods from top of stem. Sepals and petals dark reddish-brown to purple—often appear solidly colored. Dorsal sepal arched over slipper; lateral sepals joined, sit under lip; lateral petals tightly twisted, spreading. Lip an inflated pouch less than 1.2 inches (3 cm) long,

deep yellow with reddish-purple markings especially the underside; variably marked at lip opening and inside.

Leaves: 3 to 6 evenly spaced, oval blades alternately clasp stem. Leaves are bright green, ribbed and spreading, up to 7 inches (18 cm) long.

Similar Species: Unlike similar Large Yellow Ladyslipper, it rarely occurs in upland habitats, is quite fragrant and displays sparse pubescence, smaller flowers and darker colored sepals and petals.

Reproduction: Pollinators unconfirmed, likely small bees. Reproduces vegetatively along spreading rhizomes.

Range: Alaska east to Newfoundland, south in mountains to California and Colorado, south to Iowa, Illinois and New Jersey.

Where to Look: Most easily found in open coniferous forests with moist, rich soils. Also in more difficult to search habitats (fens, thickets and streambanks.) Often in compact, photogenic groups of a dozen or more blossoms, so don't forget your camera!

Large Yellow Ladyslipper
Cypripedium parviflorum var. pubescens

| APRIL | MAY | JUNE | JULY | AUG | SEPT | OCT |

Moist, upland deciduous forest, wooded swamps, meadows, bogs & fens.

Nature Notes:

Specific name drawn from Latin, *parviflorum* meaning 'small flower.'

Formerly considered part of *Cypripedium calceolus*, which occurs in Eurasia, and known as *Cypripedium calceolus var. pubescens*.

Most widely utilized medicinal ladyslipper in North America. Used by most Native American tribes of Eastern North America to treat a wide variety of ailments: anxiety, convulsions, colds, delirium, insomnia, fever, headache, menstrual cramps, pain, sedative AND stimulant (?!), tension, tremors and tuberculosis.

Widespread, familiar and popular orchid of upland forests, wetlands and savannas.

Other Names: Greater Yellow Lady's-slipper, Yellow Ladyslipper, Common Yellow Ladyslipper.

Description: 7 to 30 inches (18–75 cm).

Stout stem rises from a thick, spreading rhizome. Capsule large, up to 2 inches (4 cm) long, ribbed ellipsoid topping stem, persists through winter.

Flowers: Lone (rarely 2) glossy yellow flower nods from top of stem. Sepals and petals highly variable—greenish-yellow lightly marked with purplish-brown spots or stripes. Dorsal sepal arches over slipper opening; lateral sepals joined, sit directly under lip; lateral petals lightly twisted, spreading. Lip an inflated pouch up to 2.5 inches (6 cm) long, deep yellow with reddish markings inside.

seed capsule

Leaves: 3 to 6 evenly spaced, pointed ovals alternately clasp the stem. Bright green, ribbed and spreading, up to 8 inches (20 cm) long.

Similar Species: Small Yellow Ladyslipper, only other yellow ladyslipper in North Woods, has smaller slipper and thinner, dark reddish-brown to maroon sepals and petals. Most plants are discernible, extreme examples may not be.

Reproduction: Pollinated by small bees, notably andrenid and halictid groups. Vegetatively by spreading rhizomes.

Range: Widespread; Alaska east to Newfoundland, south to Arizona, Texas and Georgia.

Where to Look: Just about anywhere with rich soils—roadside ditches to mature forests—across the North Woods. Widespread abundance makes them an attractive target. Remember, collect only memories and photos!

Minn.

Wisc.

Mich.

Showy Ladyslipper
Cypripedium reginae

APRIL	MAY		AUG	SEPT	OCT

Wet; open forested swamps, bogs, fens, meadows & roadside ditches.

Nature Notes:

Specific *reginae* is Latin meaning 'queen,' fitting name for such a royal orchid.

Named Minnesota's state flower in 1902.

While Prince Edward Island selected it their provincial flower in 1947, its rarity on the island prompted them to replace it with Pink Ladyslipper as their floral emblem.

In its first year it may only grow as big as a pencil point, taking 14 to 17 years before its first blooms appear.

Large, striking, indeed showy orchid whose North Woods haunts are a stronghold for the species.

Other Names: Showy Lady's-slipper, Queen Lady's-slipper, Pink-and-white Ladyslipper.

Description: 8 to 36 inches (20–91 cm).

Burly stems, often 25 or more, rise from a knotty, spreading rhizome with many cordlike roots. Capsule large ribbed ellipsoid, up to 2 inches (5 cm) long, tops stem. Dried remnants of flowers often remain.

Flowers: 1 to 2 (rarely 3) large, elegant pink and white flowers nod from top of stem. Sepals and petals snowy white. Dorsal sepal ovate, arched over slipper; lateral sepals joined, sit under lip; lateral petals narrower and spreading. Lip an inflated pouch up to 2.2 inches (5.5 cm) long with circular, inrolled opening. Velvety white flushed with light pink to deep fuchsia; interior

rare white form

seed capsule

marked with purplish spots and lines. Rare all pink or white color forms occur (see photo above).

Leaves: 3 to 12 pleated, pointed ovals alternately climb the stem. Finely pubescent, heavily veined and spreading, up to 10 inches (26 cm) long.

Similar Species: Largest of ladyslipper orchids, blossoms unmistakable.

Reproduction: Primarily by bees (see page 13), confirmed pollinators include leaf-cutter bees and syrphid flies. Reproduces mainly via spreading rhizomes.

Range: Saskatchewan east to Newfoundland, south to Arkansas and North Carolina.

Where to Look: The best we've seen? Two northern Minnesota drives: Lady Slipper Scenic Byway—CR 39 south of Blackduck—has huge numbers in roadside ditches; Wildflower Route along MN Hwy 11 between Greenbush and Baudette trumps it—Minnesota DNR estimates over 800,000 Showy Ladyslippers—that's better than 10,000 per mile!

Broadleaf Helleborine
Epipactis helleborine

| APRIL | MAY | JUNE | JULY | AUG | SEPT | OCT |

Deciduous woods and roadsides, invasive in gardens and parks.

Nature Notes:

Twenty-five species of this Old World native can be found across Europe, Asia and Africa.

In areas of Wisconsin *Epipactis* has spread so aggressively that it is considered an unwanted invasive species. They have even been found growing through the cracks in concrete sidewalks!

This non-native, introduced species was first discovered near Syracuse, New York in 1878

Other Names: Broad-leaved Helleborine, Helleborine, Common Helleborine.

Description: 12 to 36 inches (30–90 cm).

Flowers: As many as 50 small, drooping, stalked flowers atop a one-sided raceme. Less than 1 inch (2.5 cm), greenish-purple lip is constricted in the middle, concave with the outer portion darker purple, petals and sepals are dull green and purple. Color can vary a great deal from pale green to dark purple/brown. Several stems may arise from a single root.

Leaves: 3 to 10, alternate, clasping, ribbed leaves becoming smaller further up the plant.

Similar Species: None, although the leaves may superficially resemble those of *Cypripediums*.

Reproduction: Easily spreads by seeds, it has escaped from cultivation and spread across the country.

Range: This European native has naturalized throughout the Northeastern portion of the US and Canada, south to North Carolina and west to Minnesota. They can also be found in Montana, Colorado, New Mexico and Pacific coastal states.

Where to Look: Usually found under a canopy of trees or along moist riverbanks, but in the North Woods it is possible to find them sprouting in gardens across northern Wisconsin.

Showy Orchis
Galearis spectabilis

APRIL	MAY	JUNE	JULY	AUG	SEPT	OCT

Rich calcareous soils amid partial shade of moist deciduous woodlands.

Nature Notes:

Latin *spectabilis*, translates to showy and is the origin of the word 'spectacular,' —undeniably a particularly well suited epithet.

Listed as 'Threatened' in Michigan.

Relishing disturbed areas they're often found along trails or streamsides and steep hillsides where minor disturbances occur naturally.

Generally south of the North Woods, with only a few records from northern Wisconsin and the Upper Peninsula of Michigan.

An enchanting orchid, providing brilliant color to the dreary, early spring landscape of eastern North America's mature hardwood forests.

Other Names: Gay Orchis, Purple Orchis, Purple-hooded Orchis and Showy Orchid.

Description: 2 to 10 inches (5–25 cm).

Compact raceme of flashy blossoms grows from a short, tuberless rhizome. Capsules are erect, three-sided ellipsoids less than 1 inch (<2.5 cm).

Flowers: 1 to 8 (rarely more) pink and white blossoms line the short stem. Vivid purple to pink sepals and lateral petals converge forming a cupped hood over the column. Lip, about ¾ of an inch (about 2 cm) long, white and spade-shaped with wavy edges. Uncommonly marked with purple. Tubular spur, swollen at its tip, is about the length of the lip. Entirely white or pink flowers are rare finds.

Leaves: Typically two (rarely one or three), rounded ovals, 2 to 4 inches (5–10 cm) wide and 3 to 8 inches (8–20 cm) long, sheath the stem at its base. Leaves, smooth, glistening dark green and succulent in appearance, may appear weeks before flowering.

Similar Species: None, the striking purple and white flowers are unlike any other in the North Woods.

Reproduction: Pollination by bumblebees and other insects attracted to the rich nectar stored in the spur.

Range: Minnesota and Ontario east to New Brunswick, south to Oklahoma, Arkansas and Georgia. Generally south of North Woods.

Where to Look: We've easily found these spring beauties while searching for Morel Mushrooms in hardwood forests of Minnesota's Nerstrand Big Woods State Park, Wisconsin's Wyalusing State Park and Iowa's Yellow River State Forest. We recommend using a diffused flash for the orchids and a frying pan and butter for the morels.

Giant Rattlesnake-Plantain
Goodyera oblongifolia

APRIL	MAY	JUNE	JULY	AUG	SEPT	OCT

Dry to moist coniferous or mixed hardwood/hemlock/pine forests.

Nature Notes:

Oblongifolia derived from Latin *oblongus* 'oblong' and *folia* 'leaf' thus 'oblong leaf' an accurate description of its leaves.

Listed as a 'Species of Special Concern' in Wisconsin.

'Menzies's' in one of its alternative common names refers to Archibald Menzies, Scottish naturalist and surgeon aboard Captain George Vancouver's ship, H.M.S. Discovery, who collected many new specimens from the Pacific Northwest.

Stout, impressively tall orchid restricted to glaciated landscapes bordering Lake Superior and Lake Michigan.

Other Names: Western Rattlesnake-Plantain, Menzies's Rattlesnake-Plantain, Green-leaved Rattlesnake-Plantain, Giant Rattlesnake Orchis.

Description: 8 to 20 inches (15–50 cm).

Tall, thick and hairy stem, amidst a basal rosette of well marked leaves, rises from a creeping rhizome. Capsules erect, pubescent about 0.4 inch (1 cm) long.

Flowers: Up to 30 small, white, downy blossoms arranged in a loose spiral along one-side of a terminal raceme. Lip pear-shaped with reflexed point that's half or greater the total length of flower. Upper sepal and petals pubescent, form a hood over the lip, lower sepals arch backwards.

Leaves: Basal rosette of 3 to 7 oblong leaves up to 4 inches (10 cm), tapered at ends, with wavy edges. Dark green with only midrib sporting white stripe. Reticulation infrequent, never the extent of other *Goodyera*.

Similar Species: Its greater height, larger sized flowers and unique leaves easily distinguish it from our other *Goodyera*. (See genus note page 15).

Reproduction: Pollinators unconfirmed probably bumblebees or other small bees. Prolific reproduction via spreading rhizomes; often forms large colonies although not all plants produce flowers every year.

Range: Disjunct distribution. More common in western range—southeast Alaska to Saskatchewan, south to California and New Mexico. Rare and local in east—northern Wisconsin to northern Michigan and southeast Ontario, also in Maine.

Where to Look: Search hemlock and mixed forests near Lakes Superior and Michigan. Most easily found along Glacial Lake Nipissing beach ridges of Apostle Islands National Lakeshore. Try July and August for blooming plants. Bring your camera for the awesome scenery!

Downy Rattlesnake-Plantain
Goodyera pubescens

APRIL	MAY	JUNE	JULY	AUG	SEPT	OCT

Favors dry to moist acidic soils under aspen, birch, pine and oak.

Nature Notes:

Specific *pubescens*, describing the flowers' downy covering, is misleading. While it's fuzzier than the others, all *Goodyera* have a downy inflorescence.

Hardy, evergreen plants with individual leaves within a rosette persisting up to four years.

German immigrants to Pennsylvania called it *err-kraut*, and folklore deemed a person stepping on it would lose their way becoming lost in the forest. So watch your step and bring a compass!

A most impressive orchid; Its superbly marked leaves are a visual treat in any season.

Other Names: Downy Rattlesnake Orchis, Adder's Violet, Net-leaf, Spotted Plantain, Rattlesnake Leaf, Scrofula-weed.

Description: 4 to 18 inches (10–45 cm).

Tightly packed raceme, centered within a ground-hugging rosette of strikingly marked leaves, grows from a many-branched rhizome often forming large colonies. Dense 'rattle' of pea-shaped seed capsules supplanting flowers often persists through winter.

Flowers: Tiny, less than 3/19 inch (< 4 mm) long, downy, white, 50-plus per spike. Dorsal sepal and petals converge forming a hood over the lip. Lip roundly pouched growing to a sharp, reflexed point, like a short beak.

seed
capsules

Leaves: Showiest of any North Woods orchid! Four to 10 dark green basal leaves form a compact rosette. Arresting network of white along veins including prominent, wide midvein.

Similar Species: Scrutiny of any North Woods *Goodyera's* striking leaves will identify most plants (see genus note page 15). Beware of intergrades! *Goodyera* hybrids and backcrosses are surprisingly common. Don't get frustrated, most intermediates are unidentifiable.

Reproduction: Pollinated by bumblebees and other small bees.

Range: Minnesota east through southern Ontario to Nova Scotia, south to Arkansas, Tennessee and Florida.

Where to Look: We've found them easily while hiking in state parks and national forests in the North Woods. Look for their beautiful evergreen leaves in spring or winter when not obscured by vegetation. Return later for flower-filled skewers of white sticking up from the ground.

Minn.

Wisc.

Mich.

Lesser Rattlesnake-Plantain
Goodyera repens

APRIL	MAY	JUNE	JULY	AUG	SEPT	OCT

Cool, acidic soils of shaded coniferous bogs, mixed upland forests.

Nature Notes:

Specific *repens* from Latin meaning crawling or creeping, referring its radiating rhizomes.

We've found them growing atop moss covered cedar logs—fallen trees that have been undisturbed for more than fifty years.

Hybridization with *G. oblongifolia* resulted in the origin of *G. tesselata*.

Settlers treated colds, and earaches with a cold tea made from leaves.

Our smallest *Goodyera*, a dainty orchid of dark, mossy woodlands whose handsome, strikingly marked leaves rival its flowers.

Other Names: Dwarf Rattlesnake Plantain, Creeping Rattlesnake Plantain.

Description: 2 to 8 inches (5–20 cm).

Loose raceme, with blossoms along one side or loose spiral, centered within a ground-hugging rosette. Small, egg-shaped seed capsules supplant flowers, often persisting through winter.

Flowers: Small, $1/12$ inch (about 3 mm), downy, white, up to 25 per stem. Dorsal sepal and petals converge erecting a hood over the lip. Lip is pouched terminating in a reflexed point.

Leaves: Plant's most distinctive feature! Basal rosette of pointed egg-shaped, dark blue-green leaves scribed with an eye-catching web of whitish tracing along veins.

seed capsules

Similar Species: While all North Woods *Goodyera* exhibit the same basic features, scrutiny of their leaves will separate most. (See genus note page 15). Beware of intergrades! *Goodyera* hybrids and backcrosses are surprisingly common. Don't get frustrated, many intermediates are unidentifiable in the field.

Reproduction: Flowers emit sweet scent attractive to both moths and butterflies, also pollinated by bumblebees. Forms extensive colonies of new rosettes from spreading rhizomes.

Range: Circumboreal. Northern Eurasia, Alaska east to Newfoundland, south in Rockies to New Mexico. Minnesota across Great Lakes to Maine, south in Appalachians to North Carolina.

Where to Look: Cool, dark bogs and forests, especially mossy coniferous forests, are your best bet, though we have found a few in old pine plantations. Its striking leaves are often hidden under needles or leaves. Easier to find in late summer when their one-sided flower spikes rise above the forest floor.

Checkered Rattlesnake-Plantain
Goodyera tesselata

APRIL	MAY	JUNE	JULY	AUG	SEPT	OCT

Dry sandy soil; conifers & mixed woods, likes pine needle duff.

Nature Notes:

Specific *tesselata* drawn from Latin meaning 'checkered' or 'mosaic-like' in describing the contrasting venation pattern of the leaves.

Has its origin as hybrid offspring of *G. pubescens* and *G. oblongifolia*. A hybrid so successful that it has outpaced one of its parent species, becoming common in Minnesota while *G. oblongifolia* has yet to be found in the state!

Shade doting orchid confined to relict path of Eastern North America's glaciers.

Other Names: Checkered Rattlesnake Orchis, Tesselated Rattlesnake-Plantain, Loddiges's Rattlesnake-Plantain.

Description: 5 to 14 inches (1–35 cm).

Loosely filled raceme, centered within a turf-clinging rosette of variably marked leaves, grows from a branching rhizome

Flowers: Loose spiral or one-sided spike of up to 45 pea-sized, downy, white blossoms. Lip pouched with elongated, blunt, spout-like tip. Upper sepal and petals cupped over the lip, lower sepals gently flared.

Leaves: 3 to 8 basal, pale blue-green leaves typically 1 to 2 inches (2.5–5 cm) in length forming a rosette. Leaves evergreen, oblong, softly

seed
capsules

pointed and variably overlaid with white netting marking veins.

Similar Species: While all North Woods *Goodyera* have similarities, careful study of their leaves will identify most plants (see genus note page 15). Hybrids and backcrosses are common in our region—with *G. tesselata* itself originating as a hybrid!

Reproduction: Pollinators unconfirmed, believed to be bumblebees.

Range: Manitoba east to Newfoundland, south to Minnesota, Ohio and Maryland. Nearly endemic to glaciated areas of Great Lakes, NE United States and adjacent Canada.

Where to Look: Conifer loving species often found in pine plantations as heavy shade and little competing vegetation offer ideal conditions. We've had great luck in Chippewa, Superior, Chequamegon and Nicolet National Forests. Easy to search, easy to find (when present) and even easier to pick up ticks!

Minn.

Wisc.

Mich.

Club-spur Orchid
Gymnadeniopsis (Platanthera) clavellata

| APRIL | MAY | JUNE | JULY | AUG | SEPT | OCT |

Sphagnum swamps, bogs & floating mats amid stunted spruce/tamarack.

Nature Notes:

Specific drawn from Latin *clava* meaning 'club' and *clavellatus* meaning 'club shaped' describing the clavate or club-shaped spur.

Listed as a 'Species of Special Concern' in Minnesota.

Genus and species names are well traveled for this orchid. Since it was first described in 1803 it's endured more than a dozen name changes!

Rare hybrid with White Fringed Orchid has been described from Michigan.

Charming, enigmatic and variably twisted orchid of sphagnum meadows, lake margins and forested peatlands.

Other Names: Green Wood-Orchid, Little Club-spur Orchid, Small Green Fringed-Orchid, Small Green Wood-Orchid, Woodland Orchid.

Description: 4 to 14 inches (10–35 cm).

Smooth stem rises from spreading roots. Capsules stout ellipsoids less than ½ inch (12 mm) long.

Flowers: 5 to 15 (rarely more) pea-sized blooms top a loose raceme. Greenish-white to yellowish-green flowers have a topsy-turvy look as they twist slightly more or less than a level 180 degrees. Dorsal sepal and petals cupped over column; lateral petals erect, spreading. Lip oblong, with three shallow lobes at tip. Spur obvious, longer than flower, up to ½ inch (13 mm) long, thickened at tip.

seed capsules

Leaves: Single (rarely 2) large, up to 7 inches (18 cm) long, pointed oblong shaped leaf clasps the stem near or just below its midpoint (may appear basal when buried in deep sphagnum.) 1 to 3 small, bladeless bracts present above leaf.

Similar Species: Confusion with Blunt-leaf Orchid (also one leaf) is possible. Easily told by lip shape—elongated, tapering to narrow tip, pointing downward is Blunt-leaf, rectangular oblong with three small lobes on front edge, often twisted sideways, is Club-spur.

Reproduction: Generally self-pollinating; pollinators unknown but hybrids exist, proving that cross-pollination does occur.

Range: Minnesota east to Newfoundland, south to Texas and northwest Florida.

Where to Look: Swamps of scrubby Black Spruce and Tamarack with ground cover of sphagnum—search areas between thicker stands of trees. Often associates with Rose Pogonia, Grass Pink and Bog Buckbean.

Minn.

Wisc.

Mich.

Lily-leaved Twayblade
Liparis liliifolia

| APRIL | MAY | JUNE | JULY | AUG | SEPT | OCT |

Rich acidic soils; moist woods, stream banks, pine plantations.

Nature Notes:

Specific *liliifolia* means 'lily-leaf' for its leaves which can be similar in appearance to those of some lilies.

Listed as a 'Species of Special Concern' in Michigan.

Well known for widely fluctuating populations, often following changes in the disturbed habitats where they grow. Large, established colonies have been known to decline rapidly over only a few years.

Charming, colorful yet inconspicuous orchid of shaded forests mainly south of the North Woods.

Other Names: Brown Wide-lip Orchid, Large-leaved Twayblade, Purple Twayblade, Mauve Sleekwort.

Description: 3 to 10 inches (8–25 cm).

Squat terminal raceme rises from current year's bulbous corm. Capsules diagnostic; erect ellipsoids about one half inch (1.5 cm) long, veins distinctly winged on stems about as long as capsule.

Flowers: Up to 30 small purple and green flowers per plant. Lateral petals purplish, threadlike and drooping. Sepals narrow and green. Lip translucent brownish/purple with purple veins, darker centrally; wide, flat, about ½ inch (1.5 cm) long and pointed at tip. Column arches over base of lip.

Leaves: Two to three shiny-green, broad ovals, strongly keeled up to six inches (15 cm) long, sheathing the pseudobulb and stem at its base.

Similar Species: Loesel's Twayblade somewhat similar but has narrower leaves and capsules with shorter stems—about half as long as capsule; not likely to be confused when blooming.

Reproduction: Pollinators unconfirmed, probably flies. Not self fertilizing, fruit production is uncommon as cross-pollination is required for viable seed production.

Range: Minnesota and southern Ontario east to New Hampshire, south to eastern Oklahoma and northern Georgia. Generally south of the North Woods; notable records from Itasca County, Minnesota, Leelanau County, Michigan and Oconto County, Wisconsin.

Where to Look: Not to be expected in North Woods. It's nonspecific habitat requirements, preference for disturbed sites and acidic soils make pine plantations good sites to search.

Loesel's Twayblade
Liparis loeselii

APRIL	MAY	JUNE	JULY	AUG	SEPT	OCT

Moist/wet ditches, fens, forests, floating mats, meadows, sandy shores.

Nature Notes:

Specific honors Johann Loesel, German author, botanist and professor of the early 17th century.

Can be volatile and short-lived, swiftly increasing or vanishing as habitat changes occur.

Individuals situated in sunny locales are typically more yellow in coloration than those found in semi-shaded sites.

Native Americans created an infusion from the roots used to treat urinary problems.

Widespread, but small and oft hidden, yellow-green orchid; blends well with its surroundings.

Other Names: Yellow Wide-lip Orchid, Fen Orchis, Bog Twayblade, Green Twayblade.

Description: 3 to 10 inches (8–26 cm).

Squat terminal raceme rises from current year's bulbous corm. Capsules diagnostic; erect, winged ellipsoids less than one half inch (<1.3 cm) long on stems about half as long as capsule.

Flowers: Loose raceme brandishing up to 25 small, yellowish-green flowers. Lip oblong and arched, folded into shallow scoop to its mid-point. Petals threadlike, outspread and curved. Sepals narrow, pointed and folded lengthwise.

Leaves: Two erect, shiny yellow-green leaves, lance-like and keeled, sheath the pseudobulb and stem at its base. Narrower than other

seed capsules

North Woods *Liparis*, up to 6 inches (16 cm) long, less than 2 inches (< 5 cm) wide and gently pointed at tip.

Similar Species: Lily-leaved Twayblade somewhat similar but has broader leaves and capsules with longer stems—about as long as capsule; not likely to be confused when blooming.

Reproduction: Self fertilizing, utilizes rain-assisted pollination. Falling rain hits the arched lip which deflects droplets toward the anther striking the pollinia knocking pollen onto the stigma.

Range: Europe. British Columbia east to Nova Scotia, south to Arkansas, Mississippi and in Appalachians to North Carolina.

Where to Look: Generally, sunny locations along wet sandy shores, ditches, fens, bogs or disturbed areas. Prefers little competing vegetation. While widespread and occupying a wide range of habitats, its low key bearing makes them easy to overlook. We've had good luck in early-successional forest openings and mine pits.

Auricled Twayblade
Listera auriculata

APRIL	MAY	JUNE	JULY	AUG	SEPT	OCT

Wet, sandy soils under alders, along streams & shores of Lake Superior.

Nature Notes:

Specific *auriculata* means little ear, alluding to the ear-like projections (auricles) at the lip's base.

One of the rarest orchids in the North Woods. Colonies often ephemeral and consist of only a few individuals. Listed as 'Endangered' in Minnesota and Wisconsin and 'Species of Special Concern' in Michigan.

Listera x veltmanii (only hybrid between North American twayblades) with features intermediate between its parent species *L. auriculata* and *L. convallarioides*, has been found in Wisconsin, Ontario and Michigan.

Elusive and scarce phantom of wet flood plain and ice-scoured shores along our northernmost streams, rivers and lakes.

Other Names: None.

Description: 2 to 10 inches tall (5–25 cm).

Pale green stem, pubescent above the leaves but not below, grows from cluster of fibrous roots. Capsules are small ellipsoids.

Flowers: Terminal raceme topped by 5 to 16 small greenish flowers. Sepals and petals narrow, curving back to expose lip. Lip rectangular, narrowed in middle, slightly forked forming two short, rounded lobes. Auricles at lip base pinch inward grasping the column.

Leaves: Two opposing, egg-shaped leaves attach at stem's midpoint. Note, in deep sphagnum, leaves laying near the surface may look basal.

Similar Species: Two-leaved *Listera* easily told from other 'little green orchids' which have only one. North Woods twayblades easily separated by lip shape (see page 16), only moderately notched, more uniform width and distinctive auricles at base clinch its identification.

Reproduction: Much about this rare species' biology is unknown, e.g. does it rely on fungi for germination and growth? Short-lived. Pollination by flying insects via remarkable method unique to *Listera* (see page 17).

Range: Manitoba east to Newfoundland, south to northern portions of Minnesota, Wisconsin, Michigan & New York, east to Maine.

Where to Look: Transient nature makes relocating them difficult. Search streamsides in sand under alders or mossy banks under trees. Our best luck has been alder thickets along gravel shoreline of Lake Superior. All sightings should be reported to respective state's DNR.

Broad-lipped Twayblade
Listera convallarioides

APRIL	MAY	JUNE	JULY	AUG	SEPT	OCT

Cool, moist shade; mossy coniferous forest, bog, swamp & stream shore.

Nature Notes:

Listed as 'Threatened' in Wisconsin and 'Species of Special Concern' in Minnesota (where the only record is a Cook County specimen collected in 1924!)

Specific *convallarioides* refers to the leaves' resemblance to leaves of *Convallaria majalis*, the much loved Lily-of-the-Valley.

Common name comes from the unmistakable lip, greatly widened at its tip unlike any other *Listera* in the North Woods.

Shade loving orchid of wet, richly soiled pockets along Michigan's Lake Superior shore.

Other Names: Broad-leaved Twayblade.

Description: 2 to 12 inches (5–30 cm).

Tallest and bearing the largest flowers of all native twayblades. Smooth stem grows from a cluster of slender, fibrous roots. Capsules are smooth ellipsoids about $\frac{1}{3}$ inch (8 mm) long.

Flowers: Loose terminal raceme bears 5 to 20 yellowish green flowers. Green sepals and petals bend back away from lip. Lip prominent, light green, darker toward center. Distinctive shape— narrow at base, broad at tip and slightly notched forming two broad, rounded lobes.

Leaves: Two opposing green leaves, broad ovals 1 to 3 inches (2.5–8 cm) long (and nearly as wide!) attached near midpoint of stem.

Similar Species: All *Listera* have two leaves; Other 'little green orchids' which have only one. North Woods twayblades easily separated by lip shape (see page 16). Slightly notched lip with rounded lobes, broad at tip narrowing dramatically to a slender attachment at base.

Reproduction: Short-lived. Pollinators unconfirmed but likely small flying insects (probably fungus gnats as in other members of this genus). Pollination via remarkable method unique to *Listera* (see page 17).

Range: Southwestern Alaska, British Columbia and Alberta south to Arizona; Ontario and Minnesota east to Newfoundland and Maine.

Where to Look: Most easily found along Lake Superior in Michigan's Upper Peninsula. Can be locally abundant in Pictured Rocks National Lakeshore. Searching woods, thickets and wet areas amid the dunes of Grand Sable Banks and Dunes RNA is your best bet.

Heart-leaved Twayblade
Listera cordata var. cordata

APRIL	MAY	JUNE	JULY	AUG	SEPT	OCT

Moist sphagnum hummocks in dark cedar or spruce bogs, swamps & woods.

Nature Notes:

Specific *cordata* is from Latin *cordatus* meaning heart-shaped, referencing the plant's pair of heart-shaped leaves.

Our most widespread twayblade, found throughout cooler, high elevations and northern latitudes. Variety *nephrophylla* resides west of the Great Plains north to Alaska.

A biological oddity in that seeds ripen so rapidly that capsules rupture, releasing mature seeds, while the plant is still blooming (see two top right photos on opposite page).

Delicate, fine-featured orchid of mossy-floored boreal forests; common, but often overlooked.

Other Names: Heartleaf Twayblade.

Description: 2 to 13 inches (5–33 cm).

Green to maroon terminal raceme, smooth below leaves pubescent above, rises from creeping rhizomes. Round, semi-erect capsules (1/4 inch (< 5 mm)) appear while flowers are still in bloom.

Flowers: 5 to 30 tiny, 3/16 inch (5 mm) long, blossoms atop slender raceme. Highly variable combinations of yellowish green, green, reddish green or reddish purple. Lip deeply forked, cleft half its length at the tip, has two horn-like projections at its base. Sepals and petals ovate, reflexed and colored as lip.

Leaves: Pair of opposing, soft green, heart-shaped leaves attached just below midpoint of

seed capsules

stem. Beware! In deep sphagnum leaves may lay at/on the surface, appearing to be basal.

Similar Species: Other 'little green orchids' have only one leaf. North Woods *Listera* easily separated by lip shape (see genus account page 16).

Reproduction: Principal pollinators are fungus gnats (Sciaridae and Mycetophilidae) and likely other small insects attracted to its foul scent. Extraordinary pollination method (see page 17).

Paired leaves are half way up the stem but may appear lower when found in deep sphagnum moss.

Range: Circumboreal. Eurasia, Alaska east to Greenland, south to California, in Rockies to New Mexico, in Appalachians to North Carolina.

Where to Look: Widespread, relatively common, but easily overlooked. Sphagnum carpeted cedar and spruce bogs in regional National Forests. Get low, go slow and bring a dry change of clothes!

Minn.

Wisc.

Mich.

White Adder's-mouth
Malaxis monophyllos var. brachypoda

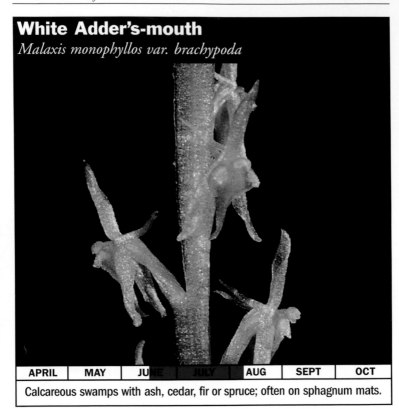

APRIL	MAY	JUNE	JULY	AUG	SEPT	OCT

Calcareous swamps with ash, cedar, fir or spruce; often on sphagnum mats.

Nature Notes:

Specific *monophyllos* taken from Greek meaning 'one leaf.'

Listed as 'Species of Special Concern' in Minnesota and Wisconsin.

Long considered a variety or subspecies within Eurasian *M. monophyllos*. Some feel differences warrant elevation to specific rank as *Malaxis brachypoda*. It is a heated debate going back to 1830!

American variety's flowers twist only 180 degrees, opposed to Europe's nominate variety that turn a full 360 degrees.

Petite, delicate and elusive orchid of deeply shaded forested peatlands, swamps and woods.

Other Names: White Adder's-Mouth Orchid.

Description: 4 to 10 inches (10–25 cm).

Slender, terminal raceme rises from a spherical pseudobulb. Capsules bead-like, more conspicuous than flowers.

Flowers: Up to 40 minute, translucent, greenish white flowers evenly spaced along fragile stem. Lip triangular, wider at base, pointed with two basal lobes projecting forward. Lacks spurs. At about $^3/_{25}$ inch (3 mm), you'll need a hand lens to view blossom features.

Leaf: Single broadly elliptical leaf up to 3.5 inches (9 cm) long. Clasping with sheathing concealing stem base and pseudobulb; appears to be higher on stem where leaf diverges from stem.

Similar Species: *Listera* species have two opposite leaves. Green Adder's-mouth has only one leaf, but flowers are distinctly different in color, shape and arrangement along raceme. Bog Adders-mouth has multiple leaves.

Reproduction: Much of life history remains a mystery. Pollinators unknown, likely fungus gnats and/or small flies.

Range: Southern Alaska east to Newfoundland, south to British Columbia, Minnesota east to Nova Scotia, south to Pennsylvania. Disjunctly in California and Colorado.

Where to Look: Widely distributed but uncommon. Carefully check thick sphagnum mats or mounds around tree roots and edges of water filled depressions in ash, cedar and spruce swamps. Best method? A slow and steady search.

Bog Adder's-mouth
Malaxis paludosa

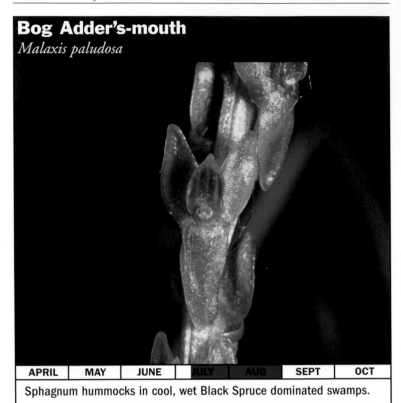

APRIL	MAY	JUNE	JULY	AUG	SEPT	OCT

Sphagnum hummocks in cool, wet Black Spruce dominated swamps.

Nature Notes:

Specific epithet is from Latin *paludosus* meaning 'swampy,' referring to its favored habitat.

Listed as 'Endangered' in Minnesota.

Our rarest orchid in the North Woods. It also bears the smallest flowers of any North American orchid.

Lacks true roots—it's the only epiphytic orchid in the North Woods—relying upon mycorrhizal fungi attached to its rhizomes for nutrients.

Clusters of up to 14 plants have been recorded in an area smaller than a quarter.

Tiny, fragile and rare orchid of open, sphagnum carpeted Black Spruce swamps.

Other Names: Bog Orchid.

Description: 1 to 6 inches (2–15 cm).

A spindly terminal raceme (with up to 35 evenly spaced blossoms) rises from a pseudobulb suspended in a sphagnum moss substrate.

Flowers: At less than $^2/_{25}$ inch (2 mm), the yellowish-green flowers are nearly microscopic! As flowers twist 360 degrees (instead of 180), the lip points upward and petals fold back. May have a slight cucumber scent.

Leaves: 2 to 5 alternate, keeled, oval leaves sheath the stem and pseudobulb at the base. Usually hidden from sight, nestled in deep sphagnum moss. Two largest leaves still only about $^3/_4$ inch (1.8 cm) long.

pseeudobulb

Similar Species: Other North Woods *Malaxis* have only one basal leaf.

Reproduction: The only confirmed pollinators are fungus gnats of the genus *Phronia*. Propagates by seed and through an unusual method of vegetative reproduction unique among North American orchids. Occasionally, the leaves produce bulbils (foliar embryos) at their tips (see photo). After a

Note the tiny bulbils (foliar embryos) at the leaf's tip.

leaf or embryo drops, a new plant (a clone of the parent) may develop. Bulbils must still be infected by the correct fungi in order to grow.

Range: Circumpolar. Northern Eurasia, Alaska east to Ontario, south to northern Minnesota.

Where to Look: A challenge for even experienced searchers. Look very closely in thick sphagnum moss hummocks in semi-shaded Black Spruce bogs. Often associated with *Malaxis unifolia,* Round-leaved Sundew and One-flowered Pyrola. Don't forget your hand lens!

Minn.

Wisc.

Mich.

Green Adder's-mouth
Malaxis unifolia

APRIL	MAY	JU~~NE~~			SEPT	OCT

Acidic soils; conifers, hardwoods, bogs, swamps, meadows or uplands.

Nature Notes:

Specific *unifolia* comes from Latin *unus* and *phyllon* meaning 'one leaf' describing its solitary leaf.

Often ripening before all the flower buds have opened, seed capsules are actually produced by few flowers (see photo opposite page top right).

Ojibwe healers used a compound created from the roots as a diuretic.

Dainty, common but overlooked emerald beauty of many habitats across the North.

Other Names: Green Adder's-mouth Orchid.

Description: 3 to 12 inches (8–30 cm) most plants about 6 inches.

Terminal raceme rises from swollen pseudobulb. Capsules ribbed beads, larger than flowers, fixed 90 degrees to stalk on stem longer than capsule.

Flowers: Dense collection of up to 80-plus tiny, less than 4/25 inch (4 mm), yellowish green blossoms on a cylindrical raceme. Flowers crowded near the top early on, inflorescence elongating as it grows and lower flowers branch out on longer stems (resembling a green bottle brush). Lip notched at its tip with two prominently pointed 'fangs' (genesis of adder's-mouth).

seed capsules

Leaf: Single ovate leaf, keeled up to 3 inches (8 cm) long strongly sheaths the stem near midpoint.

Similar Species: *Listera* species have two opposing leaves. White Adder's-mouth has one leaf, but flowers are whitish and the raceme has flowers placed singly along the stem.

Reproduction: Pollinators unknown, likely fungus gnats and/or small flies.

Solitary leaf sheaths the stem well above the moss.

Range: Throughout eastern North America; Manitoba east to Newfoundland, south to Texas and Florida.

Where to Look: Widespread and common, but rarely obvious, often challenging to find. Most easily found in open, forested sphagnum swamps. They bloom for many weeks. Ample time to learn its fieldmarks, take a hike and enjoy the thrill of the hunt! (FYI, it's common at Minnesota's Iron Springs Bog SNA.)

Minn.

Wisc.

Mich.

White Fringed Orchid
Platanthera blephariglottis var. blephariglottis

| APRIL | MAY | JUNE | JULY | AUG | SEPT | OCT |

Open sphagnum bogs, wet meadows, fens, ditches & boggy lake edges.

Nature Notes:

Specific derived from Greek *blepharis* meaning eyelash or fringed and *glottis* for mouth-like, yielding a fitting name meaning 'fringe-tongued.'

In New Jersey it grows in pine barrens, where its showy white flowers earn the descriptive moniker "Prince of the Pinelands."

Similar southern variety *P. b. conspicua*, is larger with tremendously long spurs—twice the length of the blossom itself.

Ornate, large and luminous orchid of Lower Michigan's damp meadows and open bogs.

Other Names: Northern White Fringed Orchis.

Description: 8 to 24 inches (20–61 cm).

Crowded terminal raceme of 20 to 45 angelic white flowers tops a leafy stalk.

Flowers: About 1.5 inches (3.8 cm) long with prominent curving, tubular spur. Lateral petals not fringed while unlobed lip is elongated and heavily fringed. Upper sepal cupped, forming a helmet-like hood over the column.

Leaves: 2 to 4; green, keeled, narrow, up to 8 inches (20 cm) long, sheath the stem below becoming smaller up the stalk.

Similar Species: Fringed lip but unfringed lateral petals separate it from all orchids with fringed blossoms (all three petals fringed).

Reproduction: Michigan studies showed pollination by moths, butterflies and bumblebees. In Maine, only diurnal pollinators were documented, primarily butterflies (skippers, whites and sulphurs) and bees. Ohio surveys revealed pollination by nocturnal moths. Unfortunately, they're inactive when overnight temperatures fall below 59 degrees F (15 C). A factor limiting this orchid's northward distribution.

Range: Michigan east through southern Ontario and Great Lakes states to Newfoundland, south to Maryland. One disjunct historic record from Illinois.

Where to Look: In North Woods is restricted to Michigan's northern Lower Peninsula. Check open areas of Black Spruce/Tamarack bogs with sphagnum or floating bogs in late July. Often associated with cranberries and sedges. Bring tall, waterproof boots or extra socks!

Tall White Bog-Orchid
Platanthera dilatata var. dilatata

APRIL	MAY	JUNE			SEPT	OCT

Open, wet; bogs, coniferous swamps, ditches, sedge meadows & seeps.

Nature Notes:

Specific from Latin *dilatata* meaning 'widen,' 'broaden,' 'spread' or 'dilate' describing the lip which is roundly dilated at its base.

Listed as a 'Species of Special Concern' in Wisconsin.

P. dilatata and *P. aquilonis* are ancestral 'parents' of *P. huronensis*, once thought to be the hybrid *Platanthera X media*.

Tall, radiant white and sweet smelling orchid of sun-filled wet meadows, muskeg, peatlands and swamps.

Other Names: Scentbottle, Bog Candles, Bog Orchid, Boreal Bog-Orchid, Leafy White Orchis, Tall White Bog-Orchis, White Bog-Orchid.

Description: 10 to 40-plus inches (25–100+ cm).

Tall, smooth stem rises from thick, fleshy roots. Capsules erect ellipsoids along upper stem.

Flowers: 10 to 75-plus dime-sized, brilliant white flowers top a terminal raceme. Dorsal sepal and petals cupped over column; lateral sepals bent, outspreading. Lip roundly dilated at base tapering to blunt tip. Greenish, slightly clubbed spur, more or less equal to lip in length, curves backward.

seed capsules

Leaves: 3 to 8 tapered, dark green blades, up to 10 inches (25 cm) long, sheath the stem. Spreading leaves become smaller, reducing to bracts, as they climb the stem.

Similar Species: Told from other *Platanthera* by its pure white flowers, lip that's dilated at its base, slender spur about the same length as lip and typical scent of cloves.

Reproduction: Bees, butterflies and moths have been identified as pollinators.

Range: Alaska across Canada to Newfoundland, south in western mountains to California and New Mexico, Minnesota east to Maine, south to Iowa, Illinois and Pennsylvania.

Where to Look: Often found with sedges, pitcher plants and sundews in open fens, floating sedge mats and cedar or spruce swamps. In our experience, generally not in heavy sphagnum. All these haunts shelter loads of neat things, pack your bog shoes and give it a go!

Minn.

Wisc.

Mich.

Tubercled Orchid
Platanthera flava var. herbiola

APRIL	MAY	JUNE	JULY	AUG	SEPT	OCT

Wet; sedge meadows, bog and swamp edges, alder thickets, ditches.

Nature Notes:

Specific from Latin *flava* meaning 'yellow' describing its flowers; varietal *herbiola* is from Latin meaning 'little plant,' an accurate description; Tubercled Orchid for the swollen growth or tubercle on the lip.

A species of conservation concern throughout the region, listed as 'Endangered' in Minnesota and 'Threatened' in Wisconsin.

Smaller bracted *P. flava* var. *flava*, a variety more southern in distribution, occurs south of the North Woods.

Widespread, yet rare, nondescript green orchid of undisturbed wetland habitats.

Other Names: Pale-Green Orchid, Pale Green Orchis, Tubercled Rein-orchid.

Description: 4 to 23 inches (10–58 cm).

Smooth stem rises from a tuberous rhizome. Capsules ellipsoids less than ½ inch (10 mm).

Flowers: 15 to 50 tiny green to yellowish-green flowers top a terminal raceme, each subtended by a bract longer than the floret. Dorsal sepal and petals cupped over column, lateral sepals reflexed. Lip oblong, two pointed lobes at base. Obvious, upright tubercle rises from center of lip near its base, short spur curves below.

Leaves: 2 to 5 narrow, lance-shaped blades, up to 7 inches (18 cm) long, strongly sheath the stem, become reduced to pointed bracts above.

seed
capsules

Similar Species: Confusion might occur with one of the bog orchids, but even a quick look at a blossom reveals the prominent bump on the arrowhead-shaped base of the lip unique to this orchid

Reproduction: Pollination by mosquitos and pyralid moths confirmed. Spreads vegetatively along rhizomes. Odd tubercle rising from base of lip acts as a speed bump. Instead of coming in centrally between the pollinia, insects go around the tubercle, entering the flower from the sides, directly toward either pollinia, aiding pollination.

Range: Minnesota east to Nova Scotia, south to Missouri, Georgia and North Carolina.

Where to Look: A real challenge—it's rare, uses variable habitats and is inconspicuous to boot! Try a July search of a wet meadow or edges of marshes, swamps or lakeshores with sandy or peaty soil. Remember, degraded habitats don't support these orchids. Let us know when you find one!

Minn.

Wisc.

Mich.

Hooker's Orchid
Platanthera hookeri

| APRIL | MAY | JUNE | JULY | AUG | SEPT | OCT |

Dry to moist coniferous or mixed forests and pine barrens.

Nature Notes:

Specific honors Sir William Jackson Hooker (1785-1865) prominent English botanist, professor and director of London's Royal Botanical Gardens at Kew.

Listed as a 'Species of Special Concern' in Wisconsin.

Touted by folk medicine as a cure for bruises, soreness and to strengthen weak lungs.

Long-lived, odd-flowered but thoroughly captivating orchid of pine woodlands and swamps.

Other Names: Hooker's Rein-Orchid, Pad-leaf Orchid.

Description: 4 to 20 inches (10–50 cm).

Smooth, leafless stem rises from thick, smooth roots. Capsules ridged, erect ellipsoids tightly bunched along upper third of stalk.

Flowers: 5 to 27 nickel-sized yellowish-green flowers top a terminal raceme. Similarly colored dorsal sepal and petals form a cupped hood above the lip. Lip up to ¾ inch (19 mm) long, triangular and pointed, curves up at tip. Lateral petals bent sharply back. Profile resembles old-time block-ice tongs or business end of a logger's cant hook. Tapered, pointed spur, up to an inch (25 mm) long, jutting from rear of lip hangs down.

seed capsules

Leaves: Pair of large, up to 6 inches (15 cm) long, basal, opposite and spreading, leaves lay directly on ground. Green above and below.

Similar Species: *P. orbiculata* and *P. macrophylla* have similar leaves but they're distinctly paler green underneath. These same two species have one or more bracts along their stems while *P. hookeri* has none—a feature visible before blossoms appear and after they've wilted. This species' flower's upturned lip—'Hooker's hook'—is distinctive.

Reproduction: Pollinators unconfirmed, possibly noctuid moths. Like many orchids, it may take several years before first flowering. Unlike most orchids, once they mature they often flower every year.

Range: Manitoba east to Newfoundland, south to Iowa, Pennsylvania and New Jersey.

Where to Look: Leaves lay flat, often obscured, more easily found after the flower stalk has risen. Luckily, they're long-lived repetitive bloomers.

Minn.

Wisc.

Mich.

Northern Green Bog-Orchid *Platanthera aquilonis*
Green Bog-Orchid *Platanthera huronensis*

APRIL	MAY	JUNE	JULY	AUG	SEPT	OCT

Wet; bogs, ditches, fens, meadows, seeps, swamps and shorelines.

Nature Notes:

Formerly known as *P. hyperborea*, which now refers to plants occurring only in Greenland and Iceland.

This pair (or trio!) is a bottomless pit of confusion to most folks, even experts! *P. huronensis* was once thought to be the hybrid of *P. aquilonis* and *P. dilatata*. It's now known that they're its ancestral parents.

A tip: Examine living plants in the field, compare them directly when possible (see chart next page). Caution: You'll still encounter intermediate plants that defy identification.

Only recently recognized as separate species; Much about their North Wood status unknown.

Widespread, common and conspicuous across the North Woods; an identification challenge.

Other Names: Lake Huron Green Orchid, Leafy Green Orchid, Tall Northern Bog-Orchid, Northern Bog Orchid.

Description: *P. aquilonis* 2 to 23 inches (5–60 cm). *P. huronensis* can be much taller 4 to 40 inches (10 to 100+ cm). Overlap in height.

Tall, leafy stems rise from cluster of fleshy roots.

Flowers: 20 to 45, with larger *P. huronensis* having up to 75 small, greenish flowers on a lax to densely packed terminal raceme.

Leaves: 2 to 7 spreading, green blades up to 9 inches (23 cm) long, to 12 inches (30 cm) in *P. huronensis*, reducing to several bracts above.

	flower	**lip**	**spur**	**smell**
P. aquilonis	yellowish-green lip drab yellow	lance-shaped straight sides	bluntly-clubbed 3/4 length of lip	odorless
P. huronensis	whitish-green lip whiter	lance-shaped bulging sides	tubular-shaped =length of lip	scented
P. dilitata	pure white lip white	blunt-tipped base dilated	green ~length of lip	clove-like

Similar Species: See chart above.

Reproduction: *P. aquilonis* primarily self-pollinated; *P. huronensis* pollinators include bumblebees and moths in addition to self-pollination.

Range: Generally overlapping; Alaska east to Newfoundland, south to New Mexico and Iowa, east to Maine, south to Pennsylvania with *P. huronensis* absent from prairie states/provinces.

Where to Look: Occurs in virtually every corner of the North Woods. You'll want a close look at the flower parts—don't forget your hand lens!

Blunt-leaf Orchid
Platanthera obtusata subsp. obtusata

APRIL	MAY	JUNE	JULY	AUG	SEPT	OCT

Moist, cool sphagnum swamps under cedar, spruce or fir.

Nature Notes:

Specific derived from Latin *obtusatus* meaning 'blunt' or 'dull' in description of its single, rounded leaf.

Blunt-leaf Orchid is the smallest of our native bog-orchids but under ideal conditions can be incredibly numerous. It's not unusual to see hundreds of plants within a few feet of one another.

Mosquitos are a primary pollinator of this orchid.

Eurasian subspecies, *P. obtusata. subsp. oligantha*, occurs in Alaska.

Short, common but inconspicuous orchid of mossy coniferous swamps.

Other Names: Blunt-leaved Orchis, One Leaf Rein-Orchid, Small Northern Bog-Orchid, Blunt Bog-Orchid.

Description: 2 to 13 inches (5–33 cm).

Smooth stem rises from cluster of fleshy roots. Capsules erect, ribbed ellipsoids about $^2/_5$ inch (1 cm) long.

Flowers: Typically less than 15, rarely to 30, tiny greenish-white to greenish-yellow flowers on a loose raceme. Upper sepal broadly rounded, cupped above column; lateral sepals bend back; lateral petals triangular, arching forward like squat horns. Lip elongated, tapers to narrow tip, points downward. Slender, pointed spur, about same length as lip, curves backward.

seed capsules

Leaves: Lone (rarely 2) basal leaf, oval to oblong, 2 to 6 inches (5–15 cm) long. Strongly keeled with rounded, blunt tip tapering to a narrow base.

Similar Species: Combination of single basal leaf, elongated, pointed lip and pointed spur as long as the lip separate it from all other green orchids.

Reproduction: Mosquitos and pyralid moths are confirmed pollinators. In order to reach nectar stored in the spur, they must enter between the pollinia which become attached to its face. He'll carry the pollen until it's transferred to the next orchid he visits. You may see mosquitos flying around sporting pollinia glued to their heads like small yellow horns!

Range: Circumboreal; Alaska east including all Canada, south to northern Minnesota, east through Great Lakes to Maine. South in western mountains to Colorado. Also northern Europe and Asia.

Where to Look: Barely growing above surrounding vegetation, they're easiest to find in sphagnum floored cedar, fir and spruce swamps where fewer plants tower over them.

Minn.

Wisc.

Mich.

Large Round-leaved Orchid
Platanthera orbiculata

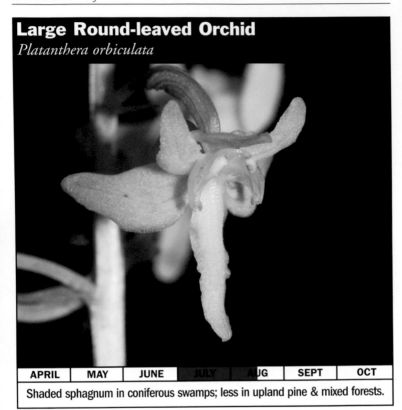

APRIL	MAY	JUNE	JULY	AUG	SEPT	OCT

Shaded sphagnum in coniferous swamps; less in upland pine & mixed forests.

Nature Notes:

Specific *orbiculata* is Latin meaning 'round' or 'circular,' describing the shape of its leaves.

Listed as a 'Species of Special Concern' for Wisconsin.

Recently recognized, Greater Round-leaved Orchid (*Platanthera macrophylla*) occurs in Northern Michigan and Wisconsin. Bloom periods are the same, and the plants are equal in all respects save leaf size and spur length. Together this species pair has the largest flowers of any North Woods *Platanthera*.

Exotic, ornate denizen of deep woods, especially mossy cedar, Jack Pine and Tamarack.

Other Names: Pad-leaved Orchid, Round-leaf Rein-Orchid, Round-leaved Orchid, Lesser Round-leaf Orchid.

Description: 6 to 24 inches (15–61 cm).

Stem rises from smooth, fleshy roots. Capsules winged, erect ellipsoids ½ inch (12 mm) long.

Flowers: Up to 30 quarter-sized, showy, white and pale green flowers top a terminal raceme. Sepals and petals reflexed and spreading. Lip narrow, tapered to blunt tip, points downward. Spur slender, up to an inch (27 mm) long, slightly clubbed and bent downward. Flowers resemble miniature green and white angels hovering about the stem.

Leaves: Two basal, opposing leaves, up to 8

inches (20 cm) across, lay flat to ground. Broad ovals, keeled, green and glossy above, silvery pale green below.

Similar Species: Recently split *P. macrophylla* indistinguishable except by spurs—27 mm or less and downcurved in this species, 28 mm or more and horizontal in *P. macrophylla*. Hooker's Orchid has similar leaves, but they're dark green above AND below. Non-blooming plants of the three are difficult to identify but *P. hookeri* has no bracts along stem.

Reproduction: Pollination confirmed for multiple noctuid moths, reported for multiple sphinx moths (family Sphingidae).

Range: Alaska east to Newfoundland, south to Washington, Black Hills of South Dakota. Minnesota east to Maine, south in Appalachians to Tennessee and North Carolina

Where to Look: Likes older forests growing in moist litter or mosses. Seldom grows in colonies. Easiest to spot these solitary plants' large, flat leaves— if you're looking down!

Small Purple Fringed Orchid
Platanthera psycodes

APRIL	MAY	JUNE	JULY	AUG	SEPT	OCT

Wet grassy meadows, fens, ditches, woods and stream banks.

Nature Notes:

Specific *psycodes* is product of a typo! It's a misspelling of Greek *psychodes* meaning 'butterfly' in description of its exquisite flowers.

Natives made a tea from its roots used to treat cramps and in childbirth.

Hybrids with Ragged Fringed Orchid (*P. lacera*) known as Andrew's Hybrid Fringed Orchid have been reported from the North Woods.

Colorful, conspicuous and exotic midsummer orchid of wetlands, forested swamps and roadside ditches.

Other Names: Lesser Purple Fringed-Orchid, Small Purple Fringed Orchis, Butterfly Orchid.

Description: Up to 40 inches (100 cm).

Tall stem rises from bundle of smooth, thick roots. Capsules small, fragile ellipsoids lined along stem's top.

Flowers: Cylindrical raceme packed with up to 125 dime-sized, lilac to purple (rarely white) blossoms opening successively from bottom to top. Sepals and petals similarly colored and spreading. Lip white at base, divided into three fan-shaped, shallowly fringed lobes. Tubular, downcurved spur nearly an inch (23 mm) long.

seed capsules

Leaves: 4 to 12 pointed, ovate blades up to 9 inches (23 cm) long alternate low along the stalk. Sheathing the stem and smooth, they climb to small, pointed bracts below flowers.

Similar Species: Only purple flowered fringed orchid in the North Woods. Rare white flowered form could be confused with White Fringed Orchid which has larger white flowers with only the lip fringed.

Reproduction: Pollinated by lepidoptera—butterflies, especially skippers, and sphinx moths (family Sphingidae) by day, moths by night.

Range: Manitoba east to Nova Scotia, south to Iowa and New Jersey, south in Appalachians to Georgia. Isolated population in Missouri.

Where to Look: Check wet, open woodlands and damp meadows. When driving through good habitat, they're often found along wet roadside ditches...but keep your eyes on the road!

Slender-spire Orchid
Platanthera (Piperia) unalascensis

| APRIL | MAY | JUNE | JULY | AUG | SEPT | OCT |

Limestone bedrock lakeshores & adjacent cedar, spruce, fir woodlands.

Nature Notes:

Species of 'Special Concern' in Michigan.

Named for Unalaska, an island in the Aleutian chain where the first specimen was collected.

Used for food by native Americans by baking the bulbs and eating them like potatos.

Inconspicuous, local and rare orchid of Great Lakes alvars on Michigan's Upper Peninsula.

Other Names: Alaskan Piperia, Alaska Orchid, Alaskan Rein-Orchid, Alaska Bog Orchid.

Description: 4 to 28 inches (10-70 cm).

Sparse but evenly spaced flowers become more dense near the top of a slender raceme.

Flowers: The 20 to 100, tiny (less than $\frac{1}{5}$ inch (5 mm)) translucent yellowish-green blossoms appear lopsided as they do not complete their rotation. Sepals show green veining and bend backwards. Lip green. Spurs are blunt, about the same length as the lip.

Leaves: 2 to 5 prostrate, mainly basal, lance-like leaves 2 to 7 inches (5–18 cm) in length yellow and die back as the plant begins to flower.

Similar Species: Thin stem with very small flowers and basal leaves absent during flowering separate it from the only slightly similar looking green bog-orchid group.

Reproduction: Nocturnally fragrant flowers attract Pyralid moths with their unusual smell, described as musky, soapy or honey-like. As is typical for orchids, a mycorrhizal fungus association is required for seeds to germinate and develop into protocorms (which linger underground for 2 to 4 years before growing their first shoots). Even after fully grown, tubers may become dormant, remaining underground for up to four years before reemerging.

Range: Primarily western North America. Alaska south to California and New Mexico, east to South Dakota. Disjunctly in Ontario, Quebec, Newfoundland and eastern tip of Michigan's U.P.

Where to Look: In the North Woods restricted to Chippewa and Mackinac Counties of Michigan's U.P. Can be locally abundant on Drummond Island.

Rose Pogonia
Pogonia ophioglossoides

APRIL	MAY	JUNE	JULY	AUG	SEPT	OCT

Open, wet sphagnum swamps, bogs, fens, meadows and floating mats.

Nature Notes:

Specific *ophioglossoides* means 'Ophioglossum like' as the emerging leaf and growing bud (photo on opposite page top right) resemble members of the fern genus *Ophioglossum* (from Greek meaning 'snake tongue.')

Rarely, in addition to white flowered forms, stems with two blossoms or flowers with fringed petals can be found. Careful study of large colonies may reveal one or more of these unique plants.

Colorful, petite, water loving orchid of eastern North America's bogs, fens and sedge meadows.

Other Names: Snakemouth Orchid, Adder's-mouth, Goldcrest, Rose Crested Orchid.

Description: 6 to 20 inches (15–50 cm).

Capsules ribbed, erect ellipsoids less than 1.25 inches (<3 cm) long.

Flowers: One (rarely two) pink to purplish blossom atop stem. Sepals and petals pink, spreading and hooded over the column. Lip with dark magenta markings and fringed tip. Center of lip covered with yellow, white or purple fleshy, hair-like bristles. Rare form has entirely white flowers, lip may display yellow bristles.

Leaves: One (rarely two) green, pointed oval sheathing the stem near its midpoint. About 4 inches (10 cm) long, strongly veined and fleshy.

flower bud

seed capsule

Similar Species: Often occurs alongside Dragon's Mouth and Tuberous Grass-Pink, but flowers differ dramatically in size and shape.

white form

Reproduction: Deceptive, produces no nectar, so pollinators (bumblebees) receive no reward for their efforts. Spreads rapidly by vegetative reproduction. Slender underground roots called stolons spread from parent plants. Shoots sent up every few inches results in large colonies.

Range: Manitoba east to Newfoundland, south through North Dakota and Minnesota to Texas, east to Florida.

Where to Look: Widespread, often found in standing water. Check floating mat edges of boreal lakes, wet bogs or swamps with Tuberous Grass-Pink or Dragon's Mouth. Also occur in wet, sphagnous swales in sandy areas like relic dunes along Lake Superior.

Minn.

Wisc.

Mich.

Case's Ladies'-Tresses
Spiranthes casei var. casei

| APRIL | MAY | JUNE | JULY | AUG | SEPT | OCT |

Dry, sandy soils of open waste areas, ditches, savanna and grasslands.

Nature Notes:

Specific, *casei*, honors Frederick W. Case, MI botanist and author of *Orchids of the Western Great Lakes Region.*

Not recognized as a full species until 1974. Formerly incorrectly considered a northern form of *S. vernalis*, a species of southern climes.

Discovered in Minnesota in 2001 by Rolf Dahle and Audrey Engels, where it's limited to mine tailing pits along a 20-mile portion of the Mesabi Iron Range in Itasca and St. Louis Counties.

Considered 'Threatened' in Minnesota primarily to habitat concerns.

Stately and uncommon orchid of open and barren areas with sandy, thin soils, particularly of the Canadian Shield.

Other Names: None.

Description: 3 to 18 inches (8–46 cm).

A thin stem covered with fine hairs supports a variable, spiraling column flourishing whitish, tubular flowers. Capsules are small, less than $^1/_3$ inch (< 0.7 mm) long.

Flowers: Single rank of 10 to 50 cream colored flowers arrayed in a loose spiral. Upper sepal and petals form a hood over the lip, all three parts pointing outward. Lip is short, downturned, about $^1/_3$ inch (8 mm) long, yellow at its base and delicately fringed.

Leaves: Basal rosette of 2 to 5 short, 2 to 4 inches (5–10 cm), oval to lance shaped leaves

usually wither as flowering begins. Upper leaves are longer, 4 to 8 inches (10–20 cm), and persist through flowering.

Similar Species: In the North Woods likely to be confused only with Nodding Ladies'-Tresses (*S. cernua*). Remember: single row, creamy flowers with yellow throats are Case's; double row, bright white flowers with white throats are Nodding.

Reproduction: Reported pollinators include sweat bees (family Halictidae) and bumblebees of the genus *Bombus*.

Range: Ontario east to Nova Scotia, south to northeastern Minnesota, Wisconsin, east through northern Pennsylvania to western Maine.

Where to Look: Found in disturbed areas with sandy soils often with other *Spiranthes*. Explore open, dry Jack Pine barrens or iron mine waste areas and tailing impoundments.

Minn.

Wisc.

Mich.

Nodding Ladies'-Tresses
Spiranthes cernua

APRIL	MAY	JUNE	JULY	AUG	SEPT	OCT

Open, wet fens, meadows, shores, ditches, woodlands & disturbed areas.

Nature Notes:

Specific *cernua* is Latin meaning 'nodding' and refers to the down pointed posture of each tubular flower's base.

Flowers have a mild floral or vanilla scent.

Considered a compilospecies, an aggressive species that plunders the genetic resources of closely related taxa via one-way flow of incoming genes. Such interbreeding produces plants from different areas displaying features of local contributing species. The result? Dizzying variability across the range of a single orchid species!

Brilliant stalks of crystalline trumpets stand as beacons amidst shorter vegetation of sandy lakeshores, ditches and meadows.

Other Names: Autumn Ladies'-Tresses, Nodding Tresses, Drooping Ladies'-Tresses.

Description: 4 to 20 inches (10–50 cm); usually less than 12 inches (30 cm).

Stem, covered with fine white hairs above, rises from tuberous spreading roots. Capsules erect, egg-shaped ovals about ¼ inch (6 mm) long.

Flowers: Crowded spike of 8 to 50 radiant white blossoms set in two to four tight, spiraling rows, each flower less than ½ inch (<1.3 cm) long. Upper sepal and petals white, forming an upcurved hood over the lip. Lip white, arches downward, edges translucent filigree resembling cut crystal. Center of base creased.

seed capsules

top view

Leaves: 2 to 6 narrow, blade-like leaves 3 to 11 inches (8 – 28 cm) long. Longer leaves are fundamentally basal with upper leaves reduced to pointed, clasping bracts. Usually present during flowering.

Similar Species: Case's Ladies'-Tresses display a single row of creamy flowers with broadly yellow centered lips.

Reproduction: Pollinated by bumblebees. Reproduces asexually by bearing minuscule plantlets sans fertilization and vegetatively by directly producing young plants from tips of spreading rhizomes—both result in genetic clones of the parent.

Range: Widespread across the eastern half of North America; North Dakota east to Nova Scotia, south to Texas and NW Florida.

Where to Look: An early successional species, populations boom amidst little competing vegetation fading away as a site matures. Best bets are disturbed areas—moist meadows, shorelines or waste areas in full or partial sun. Often persists in mowed fields & roadside ditches.

Minn.

Wisc.

Mich.

Northern Slender Ladies'-Tresses
Spiranthes lacera var. lacera

APRIL	MAY	JUNE	JULY	AUGUST	SEPT	OCT

Dry, sandy soil; Upland forests, meadows, bluffs and disturbed areas.

Nature Notes:

Specific drawn from Latin *lacer* meaning 'torn' or 'cut' in describing the fringed (think lacerated!) lip.

Currently, many taxonomists recognize two varieties; this one, var. *lacera* (blooms earlier, leaves persist through flowering and lowest flowers on stem widely spaced) and the more southerly var. *gracilis* (blooms later, leaves fade before flowering and lowest flowers on stem closely spaced.) However, varietal distinctions across our region are blurred by intergrades suggesting that treatment as separate varieties may not be warranted.

Dainty, luminous white orchid of open, sandy grasslands, pine plantations and barren areas.

Other Names: Slender Ladies'-Tresses.

Description: 4 to 18 inches (10–46 cm).

Frail flower spike rises from thick, tuberous roots. Capsules, rounded ellipsoids along top of stem, persist only a short time.

Flowers: 5 to 45 small, less than 1/3 inch (< 8 mm) long, snowy white flowers set in a single, loose spiral or along one side of a slender stem. Sepals and petals white, flourishing gently upcurved tips. Dorsal sepal and petals form a tubular hood over the lip. Lip white with green central spot or stripe stopping short of the delicately fringed lower edge.

Leaves: Basal rosette of 2 to 4 ovate leaves up to 2 inches (5 cm) long. Prominently marked

seed
capsules

by veins and usually present during flowering, although some may appear a bit shriveled.

Similar Species: One of our easiest ladies'-tresses to identify as the ovate leaves and green spot on the lip are distinctive. Keep in mind, hybrids have been reported, so potential problems exist.

Reproduction: Pollinated by bumblebees and other small bees. Flowering size can be attained in just 3 to 5 years, unlike most orchids, permitting swift colonization of new areas.

Range: Alberta east to Nova Scotia, south to Missouri, Tennessee and Virginia.

Where to Look: Intolerant of competing vegetation, often growing close to trees or shrubs. Likes sunny, open areas with sandy, well drained soils frequently with pines. We've had great luck in pine plantations or barrens and mine and gravel waste areas.

Shining Ladies'-Tresses
Spiranthes lucida

APRIL	MAY	JUNE	JULY	AUG	SEPT	OCT

Fens, stream banks, seeps, damp woods with rocky, sandy, calcareous soils.

Nature Notes:

Listed as a 'Species of Special Concern' in Wisconsin.

Specific is from Latin *lucidus* meaning 'bright' or 'shining' referring to its leaves which shine as if polished, like waxed apples or cucumbers in the produce section.

Natives used the plant in ceremonial washing of babies to assure a healthy, fast growing child. Roots were used in treatment of kidney and urinary ailments.

Saffron-lipped beauty that's our smallest, earliest blooming and least abundant *Spiranthes*.

Other Names: Shampoo Orchid, Wide-leaved Ladies'-Tresses.

Description: 3 to 11 inches (8–28 cm).

Terminal raceme rises from a cluster of slender roots.

Flowers: 10 to 20 small, usually nodding to horizontal, tubular white flowers. Generally arranged in 2 to 3 twisted ranks topping a slender spike. Snowy white dorsal sepal and lateral petals form a hood over the column and lip. Lip flares slightly with conspicuous, bright yellow center and wrinkled, white edges.

Leaves: 3 to 4 basal, lance-shaped, glossy, green leaves present during and after flowering.

Similar Species: Unlikely to be confused with any other *Spiranthes* as the lemon yellow lip and wide, shiny leaves are distinctive.

Reproduction: Pollination by small bees. *S. lucida* is unique among North American *Spiranthes* in having its nectar on the ceiling of the floral tube forcing pollinators to approach the flowers upside down.

Range: Iowa and Wisconsin east to Nova Scotia, south to Nebraska, Arkansas and Alabama, east to North Carolina. Extirpated from Kansas. In North Woods is restricted to Michigan. Unconfirmed historic records exist for Wisconsin, and it has yet to be refound in the state.

Where to Look: Prefers wet, calcareous and gravel or sandy soils. Often found in damp woods, along wet shores or old quarries and gravel pits. Your best time to search is June.

Hooded Ladies'-Tresses
Spiranthes romanzoffiana

APRIL	MAY	JUNE	JU...		SEPT	OCT

Wet sedge meadows, ditches, fens & shores; sphagnum bogs & swamps.

Nature Notes:

First specimen collected by German poet and botanist Adelbert von Chamisso. He named it for expedition financier Count Nikolai Petrovich Rumyantsev (Nicholas Romanzoff) a Russian diplomat, patron and financial supporter of scientific explorations.

Elusive, even in ideal habitats colonies are often small and short-lived.

Used by several native tribes as a treatment for venereal diseases.

Elegant and sparsely populated orchid of open, wet areas across the North Woods.

Other Names: Oval Ladies'-Tresses, Irish Ladies-Tresses (in Europe).

Description: 4 to 20 inches (10–50 cm).

Densely packed terminal raceme rises from spreading, thick tuberous roots. Capsules semi-erect ellipsoids up to 0.4 inches (1 cm) long.

Flowers: 20 to 60 creamy white flowers form three twisting rows along the stem. Blossoms tubular, about ½ inch (1.3 cm) long. Lip white with pale green lines centrally; arched, reflexed and constricted in the center producing distinctive 'fiddle-shape' silhouette. Sepals and petals united forming an upward arching hood over the lip. Sweet fragrance of vanilla or almonds.

Leaves: Three to five green, alternating and mostly basal leaves usually present during flowering. Lance shaped, up to ten inches (25 cm) long on lower stem becoming reduced to leaf-like bracts above.

Similar Species: Distinctive arching hood protruding beyond the reflexed lip separates it from all other North Woods *Spiranthes*.

Reproduction: Primary pollinators are *Bombus* bumblebees, others include *Psithyrus* and *Apis* bees.

Range: Alaska east to Newfoundland, south in mountains to California, Arizona and New Mexico, in Midwest to Iowa, east to Maine; also in Ireland and Great Britain.

Where to Look: Prefers sunny, boggy areas that remain damp throughout the year. Often hidden among horsetails or dense grasses, they can be difficult to spot. Search open sphagnum bogs, wet sedge meadows and ditches. Don't forget sunscreen and bug dope, you WILL need them!

Orchids at the Fringe

Small White Ladyslipper
Cypripedium candidum

While not a true North Woods resident, its northwestern Minnesota range includes counties along the transition zone between prairies and woodlands. Only 4 to 15 inches tall, but with a potent sweet scent. Lip, a dainty pouch less than an inch long. Blooms from mid May through June in wet prairies, sedge meadows and calcareous fens. Threatened species throughout its range. Saskatchewan east to New York, south to Missouri and Virginia.

Sparrow's-egg Ladyslipper/Franklin's Ladyslipper
Cypripedium passerinum

Subarctic relict at home on shores of Hudson Bay that occurs in small numbers along a small length of Lake Superior's North Shore. Found in protected nooks and crannies of sand dunes close to the Pic River mouth, which enters Lake Superior just north of Pukaskwa National Park, near the town of Marathon, Ontario. Up to 14 inches tall. Blooms late June to early August. Alaska east to Quebec, south in mountains to northern Montana.

Large Whorled Pogonia
Isotria verticillata

Two records from within North Woods region of Michigan's Lower Peninsula (Montmorency County—one occurrence in 1943; Kalkaska County—one occurrence in 1992), otherwise occurs south of North Woods. Usually about 8 inches tall. Blooms early—mid April to early June—on acidic soils in dry to moist deciduous forests, bog and swamp edges. Eastern North America, Michigan and Ontario east to Maine, south to Texas and Florida.

Northern Twayblade
Listera borealis

Subarctic relict that carved a niche along Lake Superior's North Shore in the wake of retreating glaciers. Can be found south of Marathon, Ontario near Pukaskwa National Park and the mouth of the Pic River, which enters Lake Superior just north of the park. Only four to nine inches tall. Blooms late June to late July in cold, wet and mossy coniferous forests, alder thickets and rocky shores. Alaska, all of Canada, south in high altitudes to Utah and Colorado.

European Twayblade
Listera ovata

Introduced. Considered a weed in Eurasia, European Twayblade is big and grows vigorously. While currently established only on Ontario's Bruce Peninsula, it has the potential to become a pest across much of North America. Four to 24 inches tall with up to 100 flowers! Blooms mid June to late July in moist, rich soil, deciduous/mixed forest edges, ditches and other disturbed areas.

Eastern Prairie Fringed Orchid
Platanthera leucophaea

Single, historic record from North Woods region of Michigan's Lower Peninsula—1924 in Cheboygan County. Tall orchid, up to 45 inches (115 cm). Stunning and fragrant when in bloom. Blooms mid June to early August in wet, alkaline prairie, old fields, open bogs, fens and peat shores. Federally Threatened. Formerly more widespread, extant Ontario east to Maine, south to Missouri and Virginia.

Glossary

Anther: Part of stamen that holds the pollen.

Anthesis: Beginning of bloom, when flower actually opens.

Autogamous: Self-fertilizing.

Acid: Having a pH less than 7.

Alkaline: Having a pH more than 7.

Alternate: Leaves attaching at successively different levels on stem.

Angiosperm: A plant producing flowers and bearing seeds in an ovary.

Auricle: A small earlike projection from the base of a leaf or petal.

Autogamous: Self-fertilized; flowers fertilized by their own pollen.

Basal: From the base of the plant.

Blade: The expanded portion of a leaf.

Bog: A wet, acidic, nutrient-poor peatland characterized by sphagnum mosses, shrubs and sedges that receives nutrients only from precipitation.

Boreal: Far northern latitudes.

Bract: Accessory structure at base of some flowers, appearing leaf-like.

Bulblet: Small bulb borne above the ground.

Bulbils: A small bulb that develops from an aerial bud Bulbils are easily detached and function as a means of vegetative propagation.

Calcareous: Containing calcium carbonate, or calcite, chalky, with a pH greater than 7.

Capsule: A dry fruit which opens, when the seeds are ripe, at several slits or holes Any closed vessel containing spores or seeds.

Circumboreal: Refers to species distribution which circles the earth's boreal regions.

Circumpolar: Living or found in the vicinity of a terrestrial pole.

Clasping: Leaves that partially encircle the stem at the base.

Clavate: Club-shaped, thickened near the distal end.

Cleistogamous: Type of flower that remains closed and is self-pollinating (see Autumn Coralroot). Fertilization takes place in unopened flower.

Column: The unique reproductive structure in an orchid flower, consisting of fused stamens and pistils.

Cordate: Shaped like a heart.

Corm: A thickened underground stem.

Corolla: The petals collectively.

Disjunct: Separated, as a population of some plant occurring at considerable remove from the remaining distribution of that taxon.

Dorsal: Above or upper.

Duff: Forest-floor covering composed of decaying leaves, needles, etc.

Endemic: Found only in one region and nowhere else.

Entire: Having a smooth margin; not toothed, notched or fringed.

Epiphyte: A plant that grows on another plant, usually a tree in the case of orchids, without being parasitic.

Epithet: The adjective, following the genus name, that forms the name of a species.

Fen: An open or treed wetland characterized by a more alkaline source of ground water than a bog.

Filiform: Threadlike.

Fringed: Furnished with hair-like appendages on the margins.

Glabrous: Smooth Without hair or down.

Habitat: Where a plant lives.

Inflorescence: The part of the plant with flowers, single or multiple The major orchid inflorescence forms include spike, raceme and scape.

Labellum: Lip, particularly that of an orchid.

Lanceolate: Lance-shaped.

Lateral: Belonging to or borne on the side.

Lip: A petal, usually of quite different shape and size to the others, normally at the bottom of the flower, or apparently so, and often, especially in orchids, of complicated structure.

Lobe: A segment or division of an organ, like a rounded protuberance on the margin of a floral lip.

Mesic: A moist and rich habitat.

Monocotyledon: With a single cotyledon or seed-leaf.

Monotypic: A genus that contain only one species.

Mycorrhizal: Symbiotic association between a fungus and plant roots.

Mycotrophic: Describing a symbiotic association between a fungus and the whole of a plant. Such an association occurs when a mycorrhizal fungus extends into the aerial parts of a plant, as in certain orchids.

Nonresupinate: Lip petal in uppermost position, as in *Calopogon tuberosus* for example. Non-resupinate orchid flowers normally position the lip at the bottom just above the column. Some genera, however, such as *Malaxis*, position the lip uppermost with the column below making the flower appear to be up-side-down.

Nomenclature: The naming of plants.

Opposite: Form of leaf arrangement; leaves arise in pairs at each node.

Ovary: The part of the pistil containing the ovules.

Ovate: Egg-shaped.

pH: A term used to express the degree of acidity or alkalinity. Measured on a scale from 0 to 14 with 7 being neutral.

Pedicel: The stem that supports a flower; can be either the main stem or smaller stems attaching multiple flowers to the main stem.

Perennial: A plant living more that two years.

Petal: One of three parts forming the inner whorl of a flower; in orchids one petal is modified to form a lip.

Pistil: The female, seed-producing organ of the flower, in orchids the pistil is part of the column.

Pollination: The application of pollen from the male organ (stamen) to the female organ (pistil).

Pollen: Spores or grains borne by the anther, containing the male element; in orchids, it is usually not granular, as in most other plants.

Pollinium; pl. Pollinia Coherent masses or 'packets' of pollen. Orchids have two, four, six or eight pollinium (packets) The number of pollinia is one of the major factors in defining a genus of an orchid.

Pollinarium: The apparatus of the orchid used to transport pollen from one flower to another.

Pouch: A floral structure modified into a pouch-like shape as the lip of ladyslippers.

Pseudobulb: Thickened or bulb-like stems (called "pseudobulbs" because they are not true bulbs) produced by some orchids to store water and food Only orchids whose habitat has seasonal periods of dryness or drought have adopted this life-saving characteristic.

Pubescent: Hairy, the hairs short, soft and downy.

Raceme: An elongated stem of multiple flowers with each floret attached by a short stem of its own.

Reflexed: Bent backward abruptly.

Resupinate: Lip petal in lowermost position on flower, the normal position in most orchids.

Reticulate: Network of veins or resembling a net, usually a different color than the leaf.

Rhizome: The woody parts of the rootstock at the base of the orchid which grows along or just under the surface of the ground or along host.

Rosette: A basal cluster of leaves.

Rostellum: A slender extension from upper edge of stigma in orchids.

Saccate: Swollen at tip, having a pouch-like shape.

Saprophyte: Plants often lacking chlorophyll; receiving nourishment from dead or decaying organic matter; needing the services of certain fungi to be able to absorb food.

Scape: The leafless stem of a solitary flower or inflorescence.

Sepal: The outermost whorl of flower segments.

Sessile: Without a stalk.

Sheath: The tubular base of the leaf surrounding the flower spike.

Spike: elongate stem of flowers; each floret attached directly to stem.

Spur: Hollow, tubular extension of the lip.

Stamen: Male part of flower consisting of filament and anther, in orchids the stamen is part of the column.

Stigma: The part of the pistil, usually sticky, that receives the pollen.

Symbiotic: Mutually beneficial.

Sympodial: A type of growth seen in some plants in which the apical bud withers at the end of the growing season and growth is continued the following season by the lateral bud immediately below.

Tuber: Thickened, subterranean branch having numerous buds or eyes.

Tubercle: A small knobby prominence.

Tuberous: Tuber-like; furnished with tubers.

Unifoliate: Having a single leaf.

Variety: Plant having minor characters or variations which separates it from the type species (var.).

Vegetative: Part of a plant not directly concerned with reproduction as the stem and leaves.

Whorl: Three or more leaves, sepals or petals arranged in a circle about an axis.

Checklist of North Woods Orchids

❏ *Amerorchis rotundifolia*	Small Round-leaved Orchis
❏ *Aplectrum hyemale*	Puttyroot
❏ *Arethusa bulbosa*	Dragon's Mouth
❏ *Calopogon tuberosus var. tuberosus*	Tuberous Grass-Pink
❏ *Calypso bulbosa var. americana*	Calypso Orchid (Fairy Slipper)
❏ *Coeloglossum viride var. virescens*	Long-bracted Orchid
❏ *Corallorhiza maculata var. maculata*	Spotted Coralroot
❏ *Corallorhiza odontorhiza var. odontorhiza*	Autumn Coralroot
❏ *Corallorhiza striata var. striata*	Striped Coralroot
❏ *Corallorhiza trifida*	Early Coralroot
❏ *Cypripedium acaule*	Pink Ladyslipper
❏ *Cypripedium arietinum*	Ram's-head Ladyslipper
❏ *Cypripedium candidum*	Small White Ladyslipper
❏ *Cypripedium parviflorum var. makasin*	Small Yellow Ladyslipper
❏ *Cypripedium parviflorum var. pubescens*	Large Yellow Ladyslipper
❏ *Cypripedium passerinum*	Sparrow's-egg Ladyslipper
❏ *Cypripedium reginae*	Showy Ladyslipper
❏ *Epipactis helleborine*	Broadleaf Helleborine
❏ *Galearis spectabilis*	Showy Orchis
❏ *Goodyera oblongifolia*	Giant Rattlesnake-Plantain
❏ *Goodyera pubescens*	Downy Rattlesnake-Plantain
❏ *Goodyera repens*	Lesser Rattlesnake-Plantain
❏ *Goodyera tesselata*	Checkered Rattlesnake-Plantain
❏ *Gymnadeniopsis (Platanthera) clavellata*	Club-spur Orchid
❏ *Isotria verticillata*	Large Whorled Pogonia
❏ *Liparis liliifolia*	Lily-leaved Twayblade
❏ *Liparis loeselii*	Loesel's Twayblade
❏ *Listera auriculata*	Auricled Twayblade
❏ *Listera borealis*	Northern Twayblade
❏ *Listera convallarioides*	Broad-lipped Twayblade
❏ *Listera cordata var. cordata*	Heart-leaved Twayblade
❏ *Listera ovata*	European Twayblade
❏ *Malaxis monophyllos var. brachypoda*	White Adder's-mouth
❏ *Malaxis paludosa*	Bog Adder's-mouth
❏ *Malaxis unifolia*	Green Adder's-mouth
❏ *Platanthera aquilonis*	Northern Green Bog-Orchid
❏ *Platanthera blephariglottis var. blephariglottis*	White Fringed Orchid
❏ *Platanthera dilatata var. dilatata*	Tall White Bog-Orchid
❏ *Platanthera flava var. herbiola*	Tubercled Orchid

❏ *Platanthera hookeri* — Hooker's Orchid
❏ *Platanthera huronensis* — Green Bog-Orchid
❏ *Platanthera lacera* — Ragged Fringed Orchid
❏ *Platanthera leucophaea* — Eastern Prairie Fringed Orchid
❏ *Platanthera macrophylla* — Greater Round-leaved Orchid
❏ *Platanthera obtusata* — Blunt-leaf Orchid
❏ *Platanthera orbiculata* — Large Round-leaved Orchid
❏ *Platanthera psycodes* — Small Purple Fringed Orchid
❏ *Platanthera (Piperia) unalascensis* — Slender-spire Orchid
❏ *Pogonia ophioglossoides* — Rose Pogonia
❏ *Spiranthes casei var. casei* — Case's Ladies'-Tresses
❏ *Spiranthes cernua* — Nodding Ladies'-Tresses
❏ *Spiranthes lacera var. lacera* — Northern Slender Ladies'-Tresses
❏ *Spiranthes lucida* — Shining Ladies'-Tresses
❏ *Spiranthes romanzoffiana* — Hooded Ladies'-Tresses

Photo Credits

The vast majority of the photos were taken by the authors—including the cover images. They have prowled the hinterlands for a combined 70 years, photographing orchids and birds, and sharing their images in books, magazines and programs. Kim and Cindy's website is www.naturescapetours.com. We at Kollath-Stensaas filled in a few holes with images from the following talented photographers.

[Photos are numbered by page and then by location clockwise from top left.]

Rolf Dahle: 35b, 54 all, 55 all, 66 inset, 68, 69, 70, 71b/c, 74, 75, 78, 79b, 88, 89 all, 95c, 114, 115 all

Marvin L. Dembinsky, Jr./Dembinsky Photo Associates: 15d, 58, 84, 113b

Hal Horwitz/Dembinsky Photo Associates: 29c, 38, 59 all, 85 all, 112, 113a, 117 top

Gary Meszaros/Dembinsky Photo Associates: 117 bottom

Skip Moody/Dembinsky Photo Associates: 116 bottom

Tom Nelson: 24 inset, 39a, 102, 103, 116 middle, 117 middle

Sparky Stensaas [www.sparkyphotos.com]: 7, 24a, 29b, 41c, 42c, 46, 47a, 49, 57, 63a, 67a, 77a, 99a, 104 inset

Sharon & Dick Stilwell: 71a

Tim Whitfeld: 81d

WISCONSIN

Chequamegon-Nicolet National Forest

Our favorite location in Wisconsin. Most of our trips to the Badger State include a visit to some part of this forest. Four disjunct units across Wisconsin's North Woods totaling more than 1.5 million acres. Enjoy a complete cross-section of North Woods habitats: uplands, bogs, wetlands, muskegs, rivers, streams, pine savannas, meadows and many glacial lakes. For the orchid lover, Tamarack/Black Spruce bogs and cedar swamps are common—as are the orchids that dwell in them!

> 1170 4th Avenue South
> Park Falls, WI 54552
> (715) 762-2461

Peninsula Park Beech Forest

An 80 acre parcel located within Door County's Peninsula State Park. A northern mesic forest of Sugar Maple, American Beech, Hemlock, birch and ironwood. Highlights include the large trees and several uncommon orchid species.

> 9462 Shore Road
> Fish Creek, WI 54212
> (920) 868-3258

The Ridges Sanctuary

Door County's Baileys Harbor is home to one of the largest wildflower preserves in America—1,600 acres. Highlights include a majority of Wisconsin's native orchids with five miles of trails to access the sanctuary. Open daily from dawn to dusk, and it's a good thing—you'll need all day to search for the 25 species of orchids that occur here!

> 8288 County Road East
> Baileys Harbor, WI 54202
> (920) 839-2802

Whitefish Dunes State Park

Another good site on Wisconsin's Door Peninsula about 10 miles NE of Sturgeon Bay along WI Highway 57. Great examples of fragile dune environments, Lake Michigan shoreline, wetlands, forested sand dunes and beech forest.

> 3275 Clark Lake Road
> Sturgeon Bay, WI 54235
> (920) 823-2400

A few favorite northern **Wisconsin State Parks** offering good orchid viewing: Amnicon Falls, Flambeau River (State Forest), Pattison and Potawatomi.

MICHIGAN

Carney Fen

This 2,325 acre marvel has an amazing diversity of habitats, including a high quality northern fen. Also sedge meadows, bogs and coniferous swamps. The recently dedicated Natural Area holds Michigan's largest and most diverse population of orchids—with 24 species identified thus far!

    Escanaba River State Forest, 5 miles west of Carney

    More information: www.michigan.gov/dnr

Cheboygan State Park

Over 70,000 acres and seven miles of Great Lakes shoreline containing a great diversity of habitats. Most interesting are the moist White Cedar swamps. Park holds many orchids, from common species as coralroots, rattlesnake-plantains, Pink, Showy and both Large and Small Yellow Ladyslippers, to rarities such as Calypso and Ram's-head Ladyslipper.

    Four miles east of Cheboygan on U.S. Highway 23.

    4490 Beach Road

    Cheboygan, MI 49721

    (231) 627-2811

Fumee Lake Natural Area

Over 1,800 acres with a number of unique features home to seventeen species of orchids.

    Fumee Lake Commission

    P.O. Box 609

    Iron Mountain, MI 49801

Pat Grogan Shelldrake Orchid Bog

An 80 acre sanctuary containing pristine examples of North Woods habitats. Home to many orchids, but the best show is in late summer when six species of orchids can be seen by the thousands.

    Chippewa County, about six miles northwest of Paradise on Vermillion Road

    Michigan Nature Association

    326 East Grand River Avenue

    Williamston, MI 48895

    (517) 655-5655

Pictured Rocks National Lakeshore

Bogs, swamps, streams and lakes provide a great deal of habitat to explore. In addition to harboring many species of orchids, these wetlands near Lake Superior are the best place to see Broad-lipped Twayblade.

    Lake Superior's south shore between Munising and Grand Marais.

    P.O. Box 40

    Munising, Michigan 49862

    (906) 387-3700

Species	MAY	JUNE	JULY	AUG	SEPT
Corallorhiza trifida		pg. 42			
Cypripedium acaule		pg. 44			
Galearis spectabilis	pg. 56				
Cypripedium parv. var. pubescens		pg. 50			
Coeloglossum viride		pg. 34			
Corallorhiza striata		pg. 40			
Cypripedium arietinum		pg. 46			
Cypripedium candidum		pg. 116			
Cypripedium parv. var. makasin		pg. 48			
Listera cordata		pg. 76			
Aplectrum hyemale		pg. 26			
Arethusa bulbosa		pg. 28			
Calypso bulbosa		pg. 32			
Amerorchis rotundifolia		pg. 24			
Cypripedium reginae		pg. 52			
Platanthera hookeri		pg. 90			
Liparis liliifolia		pg. 68			
Pogonia ophioglossoides			pg. 104		
Liparis loeselii			pg. 70		
Goodyera tesselata			pg. 64		
Corallorhiza maculata			pg. 36		
Platanthera aquilonis/huronensis			pg. 92		
Platanthera obtusata			pg. 96		
Listera auriculata			pg. 72		
Malaxis monophyllos			pg. 78		
Malaxis unifolia			pg. 82		
Calopogon tuberosus			pg. 30		
Platanthera flava			pg. 88		
Platanthera lacera			pg. 94		
Listera convallarioides			pg. 74		
Epipactis helleborine			pg. 54		
Platanthera orbiculata			pg. 98		
Spiranthes lacera			pg. 110		
Platanthera dilitata			pg. 86		
Platanthera psycodes			pg. 100		
Gymnadeniopsis clavellata			pg. 66		
Malaxis paludosa			pg. 80		
Goodyera repens			pg. 62		
Goodyera pubescens			pg. 60		
Spiranthes cernua			pg. 108		
Spiranthes romanzoffiana			pg. 114		
Corallorhiza odontorhiza				pg. 38	
Goodyera oblongifolia				pg. 58	
Spiranthes casei				pg. 106	

Titles of Interest

Here's a handful of resources that we find quite helpful for the North Woods region. We think you will, too.

Orchids of the Western Great Lakes Region, revised edition. Fredrick W. Case. Cranbrook Institute of Science Bulletin 48, 1987.

While now a bit outdated, this is one of two 'must have' references for anyone interested in orchids across our region.

Orchids of Minnesota, Welby R. Smith. University of Minnesota Press, 1993.

Along with Case, our most frequently consulted reference and a 'must read.' Also a bit dated, but packed with information.

Flora of North America North of Mexico, Volume 26 Magnoliophyta: Liliidae: Liliales and Orchidales, FNA Editorial Committee. Oxford University Press, 2002.

On-line at: http://www.fna.org/ Most complete and up-to-date information regarding orchids in the U.S. and Canada. Scientific and detailed, written in 'botany speak' so it's not easy to read, but it is complete, accurate and indispensable.

Wild Orchids of the Canadian Maritimes and Northern Great Lakes Region, Paul Martin Brown. University Press of Florida, 2006.

While the territory covered by this book is a bit east of the North Woods region, most of 'our' orchids have species accounts. Much information on identification, forms and color morphs.

A Great Lakes Wetland Flora: A complete, illustrated guide to the aquatic and wetland plants of the Upper Midwest, Steve W. Chadde. Pocketflora Press, 1998.

While it uses outdated names and taxonomy, we find ourselves using it a great deal. Often for orchid questions, more often for other associated plants.

References

Ackerman, J. D. & M. R. Mesler. 1979. *Pollination biology of Listera cordata (Orchidaceae)*. American Journal of Botany.

Arnason, T., R. J. Hebda, and T. Johns. 1981. *Use of Plants for Food and Medicine by Native Peoples of Eastern Canada*. Canadian Journal of Botany.

Bender, J. 1989. *Progress report on the ram's-head lady's-slipper (Cypripedium arietinum) project at The Ridges Sanctuary, Baileys Harbor, Wisconsin: Year three*. Unpub. report to The Ridges Sanctuary, Baileys Harbor, WI.

Boyden, T. C. 1982. *The pollination biology of Calypso bulbosa var. americana (Orchidaceae): Initial deception of bumblebee visitors*. Oecologia.

Brackley, F. E. 1985. *The orchids of New Hampshire*. Rhodora.

Brower, A.E. 1977. *Ram's-head lady's-slipper (Cypripedium arietinum R. Br.) in Maine and its relevance to the Critical Areas Program*. Planning Report 25. State Planning Office, Augusta, Maine.

Caljouw, C. 1981. *Life history and management recommendations for calypso, Calypso bulbosa, in Scraggly Lake Public Lot, T7 R8 WELS*. Report to Bureau of Pub. Lands, ME.

Case, F. W. 1964. *A hybrid twayblade and its rarer parent, Listera auriculata, in northern Michigan*. Michigan Botanist.

Case, F. W. 1983. *Platanthera x vossii, a new natural hybrid orchid from northern lower Michigan*. Michigan Botanist.

Case, Fredrick W. 1987. *Orchids of the Western Great Lakes Region, revised edition*. Cranbrook Institute of Science Bulletin 48.

Catling, P. M. 1976. *On the geographical distribution, ecology and distinctive features of Listera x veltmanii Case*. Rhodora.

Catling, P. M. 1980. *Rain-assisted autogamy in Liparis loeselii (L.) L. C. Rich. (Orchidaceae)*. Bulletin of the Torrey Botanical Club.

Catling, P. M. 1983a. *Autogamy in eastern Canadian Orchidaceae: a review of current knowledge and some new observations*. Naturaliste Canadien.

Catling, P. M. 1983b. *Pollination of northeastern North American Spiranthes (Orchidaceae)*. Canadian Journal of Botany.

Catling, P. M. 1983c. *Spiranthes ovalis var. erostellata (Orchidaceae), a new autogamous variety from the eastern United States*. Brittonia.

Catling, P. M. & J. E. Cruise. 1974. *Spiranthes casei, a new species from northeastern North America*. Rhodora.

Catling, P. M. & G. Knerer. 1980. *Pollination of the small white lady's-slipper (Cypripedium candidum) in Lambton County, Southern Ontario*. Canadian Field Naturalist.

Cingel, Nelis A. 2001. *An atlas of orchid pollination: America, Africa, Asia and Australia*. A.A. Balkema, Rotterdam, Netherlands.

Cody, W. J., and D. Munro. 1980. *The genus Listera (twayblades) in New Brunswick*. Canadian Field-Naturalist.

Cole, F. R., and D. H. Firmage. 1984. *The Floral Ecology of Platanthera Blephariglottis*. American Journal of Botany. Botanical Society of America.

Correll, Donovan S. 1950. *Native Orchids of North America North of Mexico*. Stanford University Press, Stanford, CA.

Davis, R. W. 1986. *The pollination biology of Cypripedium acaule (Orchidaceae)*. Rhodora.

Dieringer, G. 1982. *The pollination ecology of Orchis spectabilis L. (Orchidaceae)*. Ohio Journal of Science.

Duckett, C. 1983. *Pollination and seed production of the ragged fringed orchis, Platanthera lacera (Orchidaceae)*. Honor's thesis, Brown University, Providence, RI.

Flora of North America Editorial Committee. 2002. *Flora of North America, North of Mexico*. Volume 26: *Magnoliaphyta: Liliidae: Liliales and Orchidales*. Oxford Univ. Press. New York, N.Y.

Freudenstein, J. V. 1987. *A preliminary study of Corallorhiza maculata (Orchidaceae) in eastern North America*. Contributions University of Michigan Herbarium.

Fuller, A. M. 1933. *Studies on the flora of Wisconsin, Part I: The Orchids; Orchidaceae*. North American Press, Milwaukee, WI.

Gleason, H. A., and A. Cronquist. 1991. *Manual of Vascular Plants of Northeastern United States and Adjacent Canada*. Second edition. New York Botanical Garden, Bronx, NY.

Guignard, J. A. 1886. *Insects and orchids*. Annual Report of the Entomological Society of Ontario.

Guignard, J. A. 1887. *Beginning an acquaintance with wild bees*. Annual Report of the Entomological Society of Ontario.

Hogan, Kevin P. 1983. *The pollination biology and breeding system of Aplectrum hyemale (Orchidaceae)*. Canadian Journal of Botany.

Homoya, M. A. 1993. *Orchids of Indiana*. Indiana Academy of Science, IN.

Hoy, Joann M. 2001. *Listera auriculata (Auricled Twayblade) Conservation Plan*. New England Plant Conservation Program, Framingham, MA.

Hoy, Joann M. 2002. *Listera cordata (Heart-Leaved Twayblade) Conservation and Research Plan for U.S. Forest Service Region 9*. New England Wild Flower Society, Framingham, MA.

Hoy, J. M. 2002. *Listera convallarioides (Broad-leaved Twayblade) conservation and research plan for U.S. Forest Service Region 9*. New England Wild Flower Society, Framingham, MA.

Judziewicz, Emmet J. 2001. *Flora and vegetation of the Grand Traverse Islands (Lake Michigan), Wisconsin and Michigan*. Michigan Botanist.

Kallunki, J. A. 1976. *Population studies in Goodyera (Orchidaceae) with emphasis on the hybrid origin of G. tesselata*. Brittonia.

Kallunki, J. A. 1981. *Reproductive biology of mixed-species populations of Goodyera (Orchidaceae) in Northern Michigan*. Brittonia.

Keenan, P. E. 1992. *A new form of Triphora trianthophora Swartz) Ryd., and part 3 of observations on the ecology of Triphora trianthophora (Orchidaceae) in New Hampshire*. Rhodora.

Lakela, O. 1965. *A Flora of Northeastern Minnesota*. University of Minnesota Press, Minneapolis, MN.

Luer, C. A. 1975. *The Native Orchids of the United States and Canada*. New York Botanical Garden, New York, NY.

MacDougal, D. T. 1895. *Poisonous influence of various species of Cypripedium*. Bulletin of the Geological and Natural History Survey of Minnesota.

Mesler, M. R., J. D. Ackerman, and K. L. Lu. 1980. *The effectiveness of fungus gnats as pollinators*. American Journal of Botany.

Minnesota Department of Natural Resources, Natural Heritage Program. 1993. *Minnesota's native vegetation: A key to natural communities*. Version 1.5. Minnesota DNR, St. Paul, MN.

Mosquin, T. 1970. *The reproductive biology of Calypso bulbosa (Orchidaceae)*. Canadian Field-Naturalist.

Rasmussen, H. N. 1995. *Terrestrial orchids: From Seed to Mycotrophic Plant*. Cambridge: Cambridge University Press. Cambridge, U.K.

Rasmussen, H.N. 2002. *Recent developments in the study of orchid mycorrhiza*. Plant and Soil.

Richburg, Julie A. 2003. *Aplectrum hyemale (Muhl. ex Willd.) Nutt. Puttyroot Conservation and Research Plan for New England.* New England Wild Flower Society, Framingham, MA.

Robertson, C. 1928. *Flowers and insects.* Carlinville, IL.

Sheviak, C. J. 1974. *An introduction to the ecology of the Illinois Orchidaceae.* Illinois State Museum, Springfield, IL.

Sheviak, C. J. 1982. *Biosystematic study of the Spiranthes cernua complex.* New York State Museum Bulletin 448.

Sheviak, C. J. and M. L. Bowles. 1986. *The prairie fringed orchids: a pollinator-isolated pair.* Rhodora.

Sheviak, C. J. 1991. *Morphological variation in the compilospecies Spiranthes cernua (L.) L.C. Rich.: Ecologically-limited effects of gene flow.* Lindleyana.

Sheviak, C. J. and P. M. Brown. 2002. *Spiranthes.* 530–545. In: *Flora of North America* Editorial Committee (Editors). *Flora of North America* Volume 26: *Magnoliophyta: Liliiadae: Liliales and Orchidales.* Oxford University Press. New York, NY.

Sheviak, C. J. and P. M. Catling. 2002. *Aplectrum.* Page 632 in *Flora of North America* Editorial Committee (Editors). *Flora of North America* Volume 26: *Magnoliophyta: Liliiadae: Liliales and Orchidales.* Oxford University Press, New York, NY.

Smith, Welby R. 1993. *Orchids of Minnesota.* University of Minnesota Press. Minneapolis, MN.

Smith, G.R. and G.E. Snow. 1976. *Pollination ecology of Platanthera (Habenaria) ciliaris and P. blephariglottis (Orchidaceae).* Botanical Gazette.

Stern, William. 2005. *Plant Names Explained: Botanical Terms and Their Meaning.* David & Charles, Horticulture, Boston, MA.

Stoutamire, Warren P. 1964. *Seeds and seedlings of native orchids.* Michigan Botanist.

Stoutamire, Warren P. 1967. *The Floral Biology of the Lady's-slippers.* Michigan Botanist.

Stoutamire, W. P. 1968. *Mosquito pollination of Habenaria obtusata (Orchidaceae).* Michigan Botanist.

Stoutamire, Warren P. 1971. *Pollination in temperate American orchids.* M. J. G. Corrigan [ed.], Proceedings 6th World Orchid Conference. Halstead Press, Sydney, Australia.

Stoutamire, W. P. 1974. *Relationships of the purple-fringed orchids Platanthera psycodes and P. grandiflora.* Brittonia.

Steele, W. K. 1995. *Growing Cypripedium reginae from seed.* American Orchid Society Bulletin.

Thien, L. B. & B. G. Marcks. 1972. *The floral biology of Arethusa bulbosa, Calopogon tubersosus and Pogonia ophioglossoides.* Canadian Journal of Botany.

Thien, L. B. & F. Utech. 1970. *The mode of pollination in Habenaria obtusata (Orchidaceae).* American Journal of Botany.

Voss, E. G. & R. E. Riefner. 1983. *A pyralid moth (Lepidoptera) as pollinator of Blunt-leaf Orchid.* Great Lakes Entomologist.

Wallace, L.E. 2006. *Spatial genetic structure and frequency of interspecific hybridization in Platanthera aquilonis and P. dilatata (Orchidaceae) occurring in sympatry.* American Journal of Botany.

Wallace, L.E. 2004. *A comparison of genetic variation & structure in the allopolyploid Platanthera huronensis & its diploid progenitors, Platanthera aquilonis & Platanthera dilatata (Orchidaceae).* Canadian Journal of Botany.

Waterman, Richard J. and Bidartondo, Martin I. 2008. *Deception above, deception below: linking pollination and mycorrhizal biology of orchids.* Journal of Experimental Botany.

Williams, S. A. 1994. *Observations on reproduction in Triphora trianthophora (Orchidaceae).* Rhodora.

Index

Quick Orchid Finder

Other user-friendly guides from Kollath-Stensaas

Lichens of the North Woods

Insects of the North Woods

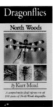

Dragonflies of the North Woods

Moths & Caterpillars of the North Woods

Butterflies of the North Woods

Spiders of the North Woods

Damselflies of the North Woods

Amphibians & Reptiles of the North Woods

Learn more about our books and authors at
www.kollathstensaas.com